PRAISE FOR *THE ULTIMATE SALES PRO*

"I have worked with many sales professionals throughout my career who believe that the main criteria to succeeding in sales is the ability to build strong relationships. I disagree. Strong relationships are important but they only get you an appointment and will not get you the sale! What will get you the sale is your ability to uncover or create customer-specific needs. It is critical to ask questions that are constructed strategically to drive your agenda in creating value for the customer. Read this book and learn powerful strategies to engage your customers and become the ultimate sales pro."

—BRUCE AUGUSTENSEN,
Senior Director, Sales, Avantik US

"*The Ultimate Sales Pro* gives you the road map to focus on the right opportunities and leverage your time and career wisely. Get immersed in this book so you can acquire the tools you need to succeed."

—TIM BROWN,
President, Moor Instruments

"Our business is up 35% over the same period last year. Your concepts are amazing and extremely enlightening. We've become 'Ultimate Sales Pros'."

—JAMES MORNAN,
Account Manager, Brookaire

"*The Ultimate Sales Pro* is an incredible accumulation of insights from a remarkable career."

—ASHLEY CHAPIN,
Producer, Business 21 Publishing

"What Paul Cherry shared with us and included in this book has had a tremendous impact on our success."

—DREW MAILEY,
Partner, Arrow Advertising

"Anyone who is serious about taking their sales career to the next step has to read *The Ultimate Sales Pro*."

—BILL SHULBY,
Former Director of Talent and
Organizational Development, Cigna Healthcare

"I live and breathe the concepts in this book because they work! Get on the path to success with *The Ultimate Sales Pro*."

—DREW MCMINN,
Regional Vice President, Springfield Electric

"We've worked with many sales thought leaders but Paul was the one who helped us increase our sales dramatically. Now you can get viable solutions to the challenges you face in this incredible book."

—ANDREW FIRTH,
General Manager, Arrowquip

"Paul's concepts are eye-opening, thought-provoking, and progressive. Dive deep and start achieving the results you deserve."

—JERRY CURRIE,
Sales Team Leader, The Hustler Corporation

"I've known Paul for more than twenty years. Unlike so many me-too sales books, *The Ultimate Sales Pro* is packed with innovative and radical ideas to catapult your sales career."

—DENITA CONNOR,
CEO Business Coach at YPO

the
ULTIMATE SALES PRO

the ULTIMATE SALES PRO

WHAT THE BEST SALESPEOPLE DO DIFFERENTLY

PAUL CHERRY

HarperCollins
LEADERSHIP
An Imprint of HarperCollins

Published by HarperCollins Leadership, an imprint of HarperCollins.

Book design by Elyse Strongin, Neuwirth & Associates.

ISBN 978-0-8144-3896-1 (eBook)

Library of Congress Control Number: 2018942033

ISBN 978-0-8144-3895-4

Printed in the United States of America
18 19 20 21 22   LSC   10 9 8 7 6 5 4 3 2

CONTENTS

CONTENTS

ACKNOWLEDGMENTS

Dedicated to my wife, Claire, who keeps me humble.

To Brooke and McKenzie, continue to do your best and pursue your dreams.

To David Byers, who has been with me all these years and always goes above and beyond my expectations.

To Michael and Patricia Snell of Michael Snell Agency. Without you, this book would never have come to fruition. You challenged and pushed me to do better, to create perfection, and I hope I at least met you halfway.

To Tim Burgard, who worked diligently with us on this book and my previous one.

To Michael Boyette, who is a gifted and talented writer and did an awesome job to take my jumbled and chaotic thoughts and weave them into a coherent and focused message of value.

A big thanks to all of you.

INTRODUCTION

THRIVING IN THE NEW WORLD OF SALES

Here's a story about two salespeople. Let's call them Ted and Nancy.

They both started their careers in the same sales department of a midsized manufacturing company. New to sales, both had to work their way up through the ranks. They started out qualifying leads and handing off the promising ones to more experienced sales reps—the job known today as *business development*. They dealt with all kinds of people—some annoyed at getting a sales call, some friendly and eager to talk, some who seemed like good prospects, and others who were simply tire-kickers. As Ted and Nancy listened, they learned about the industry and about the kinds of problems that prospects faced.

Slowly, they learned to tell who was telling the truth and who was just blowing smoke.

As Ted and Nancy sat in on sales meetings and talked to successful reps, they began to understand all the things that go into a successful sale—how to identify customer needs, dig deep, differentiate their products from those of competitors. They learned when to push forward and when to back off. They learned that sales require much more than the gift of gab.

Eventually they each got a sales territory of their own. And that's when their paths began to diverge. Ted was a solid, reliable performer. His customers liked him. His bosses saw that he worked hard. But Nancy soon emerged as a star. She brought in accounts nobody had even known about. Her customers were effusive in their praise. Soon she was closing six-figure deals while her colleagues were scratching after modest orders. She was on a first-name basis with the CEOs at the companies she served. Soon they were calling her in for advice and consultation. When a national-accounts position opened at one of her clients, they pleaded with Nancy to take the job. Now she was selling huge deals and had become a recognized leader in her industry, presenting at conferences and writing articles.

Nancy also found time to engage in her community. She served on the local business council and was elected to the school board. She cultivated a network of friends, clients, colleagues and former employees, influencers, and industry leaders.

When the vice president of sales retired, Nancy's company asked her to head up the sales operation. After giving it much thought, she declined. Instead, she started her own consulting business, which allowed her to choose her clients and control her own destiny.

Meanwhile, Ted was doing OK. He was earning a good living. He liked his clients, sent his kids to private school, and played golf on Fridays. But after ten years with his company, he was feeling simultaneously bored and beleaguered. He was solving the same kinds of problems for the same kinds of customers year in and year out. He could give the company's standard sales presentation in his sleep and had probably done so in more than one client meeting. He grew increasingly impatient with smoke blowers and big talkers. Many days, Ted felt like he was phoning it in—which was perhaps why he now found himself struggling to keep his sales where they'd been in previous years.

Ted thought about looking for a new job, but it seemed to him that he'd just be doing the same sort of thing at another company. At his current job, he had the security of long-term accounts, and making a change seemed like a risky move.

Do you know Nancy? Do you know Ted? Have you run across them in your professional life?

I've known both. In my experience as a sales coach and consultant, I've run across lots of Teds, but only a few Nancys.

Now, I don't want to suggest that the Teds of this world are unsuccessful or incompetent. They're good salespeople and, for the most part, fine human beings. Many people would envy their income and their lifestyle.

If you're a Ted and satisfied with your life, stop reading right now. This book is not for you.

But here's what many, many Teds have confided to me: They're not happy. They feel anxious and unfulfilled. They may put up a good front at work. They may still be putting sales up on the board. But they find it harder and harder to get out of bed in the morning.

And, unfortunately, I see many salespeople like Ted who end up courting disaster. They may be one phone call away from losing their cornerstone client and then they're scrambling. Or they find their industry changing, and their well-practiced sales skills and book of business are no longer enough to see them through. They see their incomes stagnate or even decline, and the comfortable lifestyle is suddenly threatened. Sometimes they respond by making risky moves—they take a new job with a promise of bigger commissions, or they start leaning on their customers to spend more without giving them a good reason to. Or even worse, they start bending the rules—clogging their pipelines with "prospects" they know will never buy, sending out invoices at the end of the quarter to customers who haven't said yes yet, trying to poach other reps' accounts, padding their expense reports.

That story doesn't end well.

Why do some salespeople end up like Ted while others end up like Nancy? It's not necessarily native talent—at the beginning of their careers, Ted and Nancy were nearly neck and neck. It's not a matter of hard work—in fact, Ted probably works as hard, or harder, than Nancy.

The key difference between a Ted and a Nancy is a matter of perspective and what they focus on. Ted focuses on selling products—getting customers to say yes. Nancy takes a larger view. She knows that selling skills and knowledge are critical to her success. But they're only the foundation. Nancy isn't just looking at how to sell a product. She IS the product. Everything she does is aimed at increasing her own value.

Once you understand that this is your number-one job, it's hard to go back to being a product-peddling salesperson. Once you start looking at how you build value for yourself, a different path becomes clear.

Nancy discovered that path early in her career. But it's not too late for Ted. I've seen plenty of salespeople transform themselves almost overnight after years of struggle. For one reason or another, they're prompted to start thinking differently about what they do. It's as if a veil has been lifted, and they can suddenly see a new way forward.

This is the path that leads to what we're calling the *Ultimate Sales Professional*. In this book, we'll explore what it means to sell at a higher level, how it differs from what you've been taught about sales in the past, and how to get yourself on that path.

THE BOUNDARY-LESS CAREER

•

Researchers confirm what we all intuitively feel: The old-fashioned notion of a career has been exploded over the last fifty years by a powerful combination of economic and social forces. We know that traditional career paths have disappeared, and that the idea of working your way up through the ranks of the corporation is as outdated as flannel suits and cars with fins.

What's replaced the corporate ladder, researchers say, is something they identify as the boundary-less career—a career that's defined by you, not your company. And here's the key point: It's not anarchy. There is still a path to success. It looks different, but studies show that people who take a deliberate approach to managing their career can thrive in this environment.

It doesn't mean you have to leave your job or company to get ahead. Successful salespeople can work their entire lives in one organization and still have a boundary-less career. It's about owning your career. The concept isn't limited to salespeople, of course, but sales careers are uniquely suited to this new reality. Salespeople are fundamentally entrepreneurial, whether on their own or working for a large organization. They're driven by results and less bounded by policies and procedures. If the concept of a boundary-less career works, everyone will see it, and smart sales managers won't get in your way.

That said, a boundary-less orientation positions you to grow beyond your current job and company if that's what matters to you. The personal value you create belongs to you and moves with you. That's what Nancy discovered. As a salesperson, she did a great job creating value for her company by selling its products. She also created value for herself by how she did it. The two are perfectly compatible.

What makes this concept so compelling for salespeople is that the drivers of success in this new world of sales are largely within your control. You don't need anyone's permission to acquire or develop them. You don't have to wait your turn or put in your time to be eligible for them. You don't have to negotiate for them in a performance review. They belong to you, and you alone. You can start building them right now, today, and reap the benefits sooner than you might have thought possible.

Now, you might be thinking: "Sounds great in theory, Paul, but it's cold out there. Can I really have a successful sales career playing by my own rules versus the rules of a big organization that can take care of me?"

One answer to that question is that companies don't play by those rules anymore, if indeed they ever did. I'm not suggesting that companies are run by coldhearted bean counters who don't care about their people. On the contrary, I've found that most managers take the well-being of their people very seriously. They want to grow and develop them and keep them around for a long time.

But what's different today is that their ability to do so is far more limited. Faced with the demands of fast-changing markets, cost-cutting pressures from investors, and the need to deliver consistently high returns, companies live close to the edge. They have to be nimble and efficient in order to survive, and relentlessly focused on value. So their number-one priority can't be your career. Like it or not, you're already living in a boundaryless economy.

Take the industry where I started my sales career, for example, directory advertising. Each regional market was pretty much divided between two major players: the regional phone company (the Yellow Pages) and Donnelly (Yellow Book). They fought tooth and claw, but overall the industry was huge, highly profitable, and stable. Companies could afford to make huge investments in their sales forces. The training was intense. The compensation was generous. The work was hard, but if salespeople were good at their job, they could expect to spend their entire careers at these companies, rising steadily through the ranks.

Once the internet came along, however, that model went out the window. As ad revenue declined, highly successful salespeople found themselves unemployed, and their specialized sales skills no longer relevant. It wasn't the salespeople's fault. It wasn't the companies' fault. The market had changed.

Veteran salespeople from just about any industry can probably tell a similar story. Wherever you look, once-stable markets are facing disruption and destabilization. These days, you have to be a different kind of salesperson to succeed.

I don't want to suggest that this new world of sales is all doom and gloom, however. There's a positive side to the story.

Researchers who have been watching these trends for decades have concluded that you can succeed and even soar in a boundary-less world of sales. Many salespeople, in fact, can do far better for themselves than they could have in a more structured situation. In a world where value drives success, valuable people will thrive and the only limit to how far they go is their own ability and drive.

The research also suggests that the boundary-less work environment isn't a free-for-all. It simply operates by different rules. According to a large metastudy, which consolidated findings from hundreds of research studies, success in boundary-less careers is overwhelmingly based on what you know.

KNOWING WHOM

•

The first set of "knowing" skills is all about your relationships. Good salespeople don't just think about how they're going to get a buyer to sign on the bottom line. They know that long-term success comes from investing in mutually beneficial relationships with buyers throughout their career.

Ultimate Sales Professionals take it a step further. They know that their success also depends on relationships outside the salesperson-customer interaction. They think about their relationships with their *customers' organizations* ("Where do I fit in to the organization's processes, plans, and future?"); leaders in their *industry* ("Who can connect me with the movers and shakers in the market?"); their own *bosses and coaches* ("How can they help me grow?"); their *colleagues* ("How can I leverage their knowledge and experience to do a better job for my customers?"); and their *own organizations* ("How can I mobilize its collective knowledge and resources to increase my value?").

WHO KNOWS YOU?

Networks aren't just about whom you know. They're also about who knows you. Great salespeople know that their personal reputation transcends the products they sell and the company they represent. Customers, potential customers, and influencers see them as a valuable resource in their own right. Ultimate Sales Pros are experts at promoting themselves and do so without apology, because they know how much value they deliver. They understand how to create a personal brand using the salesperson's most valuable tool—emotions—because they understand that the most valuable brands are those that create passion.

Whom you know and who knows you are two different things. Let's say you write a blog post. It gets 25,000 views. You'll never personally connect with more than a few of those 25,000. Yet everyone who reads that post becomes, in a sense, part of your professional network. They amplify your reach. Perhaps they'll pass on your post to someone who's looking to buy what you sell.

Perhaps your name will come up when the boss asks, "Whom do we know that does x?" Perhaps the reader who sees your name coming up on different blogs decides she really should connect with you through LinkedIn. Perhaps someone searching the web for what you sell finds your post, because so many other people have clicked on it.

KNOWING HOW

•

The next type of knowing includes your foundational skills. These are your stock in trade—the tools you use to turn opportunities into revenue. It starts with knowing how to sell—how to close a deal, how to turn around an objection, how to find new prospects, and so on.

Ultimate Sales Professionals are lifelong learners. They hunger to know more—more about their customers, their industry, their products, themselves. They constantly practice their sales skills and develop new ones. They keep up with the research and industry trends. They know more about their customers' business than the customers themselves. They ask, "What do I need to learn today to be at the top of my game tomorrow?"

They know their own limitations and weak spots and seek out mentors and experts to fill the gaps. They also mentor others, knowing that the best way to truly learn something is by teaching it to someone else. They view every interaction as a potential learning experience and continually adjust their approach to sales in light of new information.

But in a boundary-less sales career, you need to know more than sales. You need to cultivate a higher level of skills so that you can leverage your value beyond the product or service you sell.

In the directory advertising business, for example, we learned how to put together high-value advertising programs for small-business owners who felt every cent coming out of their own pocket. But those skills weren't enough when the industry imploded. How do you sell Yellow Pages ads when nobody uses the Yellow Pages anymore?

So knowing how also demands a higher set of business skills. According to the research, the most valuable skills are *occupational* skills, not *job* skills. In other words, mastering the core competencies of sales as a profession, which are transferable to other companies and products. Knowing how to help a risk-averse buyer make a decision is an occupational skill that's valuable no matter what you're selling. Knowing how your product stacks up against the competition is a job skill—it's only valuable in the job you're doing right now.

Both are essential, of course, but there's a trap to avoid here. Organizations tend to put a higher value on job skills, the skills that help sell their particular products and services. That's why they put a lot of time, effort, and money into product training. But it may mean that the company is investing less in "occupational" sales skills training—those higher-level skills that you get to take with you. If you're thinking about your personal value, you may need to seek that training on your own.

When the directory advertising business changed, I saw firsthand the value of these occupational, transferable sales skills. Among my former colleagues, a sharp division emerged. People who'd focused on job skills—learning how to sell directory advertising—were in trouble. In fact, some of the people who'd been best at selling ads now struggled the most, because their skills were highly specific to the product.

Meanwhile, those who'd taken a broader view—who'd taken a step back to truly understand their customers' businesses and the challenges they faced—were able to leverage that knowledge into selling new kinds of products and services. Those plumbers and lawyers and electricians and doctors who no longer bought directory ads still had the same problem. They needed to attract customers. Salespeople who could figure out how to solve that problem in different ways, for example, through internet advertising, SEO, sales promotions, and so on, had a customer base desperate for their help.

Others became consultants, effectively leveraging what they'd learned as *sellers* to help customers become better *buyers.* Still others used the general knowledge they'd gained about selling— how buyers assess risk and value, how to create an effective business case, how to create an emotional connection with a prospect, and so on—to sell successfully in completely different markets.

All of the people who successfully made the transition to new selling careers understood one thing: Their value wasn't based on their knowledge of directory advertising. It was based on their ability to identify customer needs and address them. That's an example of *personal* value. It isn't tied to what you sell or whom you represent. It goes with *you,* wherever you go.

KNOWING WHY

•

This dimension is about planning and strategy. If you know the *why*, you'll know *what* to do. You'll also know what *not* to do. Knowing why gives you the courage and clarity to focus on the right things and stop doing things that aren't getting you anywhere.

There are two levels of why to consider. We often think of why as huge questions about the meaning of life: "Why am I in a sales career at all?" "Why do I get up every morning and go to work?" Those are important questions, and I'll explore them at length.

But the smaller whys are equally important. "Why am I focusing on prospects in Industry A versus Industry B? Is it because they're likely to be more valuable, or is it just because that's whom I focused on in the past?" "Why do customers buy from me?" "Why do they not buy from me?" "Why does prospecting always seem to fall to the bottom of my to-do list?"

Before you spend a single minute of your precious time on any activity, know the why behind it.

Asking why also helps you understand yourself. Why do you enjoy certain aspects of sales more than others? What does that imply about how to shape your career path and what you can realistically expect to achieve?

In addition, "why" is closely connected with goal clarity and proactivity. If you know the why, you can make things happen. If you don't, you're more likely to be reactive, simply taking what's handed to you. This is an area that pretty-good salespeople often overlook. They're willing to outsource the "why" to others. They're hired guns—"Tell me what to sell, and I'll go sell it." They can make a good living, but they're always working for someone else's vision, not their own. And that can ultimately leave them profoundly dissatisfied.

Ultimate Sales Professionals excel at setting goals for themselves and others, and at turning those goals into action. *Every* action they take is designed to move them closer to their long-term goals. No effort is wasted. A lost sale becomes an opportunity to learn. A won sale becomes a platform for future growth. A casual encounter becomes a way to expand their network of resources.

Top salespeople take charge of their own planning and goal setting. They don't wait for their managers to tell them whom to sell to; they decide for themselves what kinds of customers they want and get them. They don't settle for hitting quota; they think about how to maximize their own revenue. Even when they're working within a larger organization, they're working for themselves, and their bosses love them for it.

the
ULTIMATE SALES PRO

1

DREAM BIG GOALS

How high should you aim in your sales career?

Nobody but you can answer that question. But the critical thing is to *ask* it.

In my many years working with salespeople, I've encountered several who are happy with where they are. I applaud them. But I've also encountered many who haven't really given the issue serious thought. Their goals don't extend much beyond the end of the quarter or the end of the year. "I'm too busy with the here-and-now to worry much about the future," they tell themselves. "I'll deal with it when it gets here."

The problem with that approach is that short-term goals become a stand-in for long-term goals. And short-term goals are small goals.

I believe that most people can achieve far more than they think possible. And I'm not just talking about money. I'm talking about a career that allows you to live the kind of life you want, do the work you want to do, and make the most of your skills.

So dream big. Right now, take fifteen minutes. Silence your phone. Find a quiet place. And write down your dreams. The dream you keep hidden. The one that people would laugh at if they knew. The one you've told yourself is out of reach.

It's hard, isn't it? The gap between where we are and where we want to be is not a comfortable place to be. It's tough enough to keep up with our day-to-day responsibilities. Admitting that we want more can feel overwhelming. We think of a million reasons why we can't get there. We're not in the right job. We don't have the right skills. We didn't go to the right school. We don't have the right connections. We need to put food on the table. And if we're really honest with ourselves, we'll admit that we don't want to try and fail.

I know. I've aimed high, too. And I've failed more times than I can count.

But, I've learned, there are two ways to fail. One sets you back. Another moves you forward. And the only way you can fail forward is to know what you're aiming for.

As I approached my thirty-fourth birthday, I had a lot to feel good about. I'd been in sales for ten years. Like most salespeople, I'd had some big successes and some rough patches. But overall, I was doing well. I knew how to earn a good living, and my future looked solid.

But solid was not a word that filled me with excitement. As I looked forward to the next thirty years or so, was this the path

I *wanted* to follow? Or would it simply be a path I *happened* to follow?

I'd always been intrigued and inspired by great motivational speakers—people like Zig Ziglar, Brian Tracy, Wayne Dyer, Tony Robbins. At the time, I was selling *things*. These people were selling *ideas*—ideas that made a difference in people's lives.

What a great way to make a living, I thought.

It's easy to talk about pursuing your dreams, but the reality is that there's considerable risk involved. The speaking and personal-development industry was huge. But I had no experience or credentials, apart from one public-speaking course in college and a few speeches I made when I belonged to Toastmasters. Was I really willing to move away from my comfortable sales career into uncharted territory? Wasn't I taking an awful risk?

Yes, I was willing. But I did want to minimize my risk.

TAKING STOCK

So I took four steps, which I recommend to anyone who's contemplating a big change in their career or in their life.

STEP 1: I finally got honest with myself about what I wanted. I had to think long and hard about whether this was a goal I really wanted to achieve. It was going to be hard, no doubt. Was the dream worth it? My gut told me it was. Nothing else I could imagine measured up to the idea of running my own business, selling what I believed in, and working with customers of my own choosing.

STEP 2: I had to silence that critical voice in my head. You know, the one that says, "Who do you think you are?" This is not the voice of caution and reason. It's the voice we hear, starting when we were kids, from parents, teachers, friends, family, ourselves. It has nothing to do with your actual abilities or the odds of succeeding. It's the voice that says wait your turn, don't stick your neck out, and don't get too big for your britches.

STEP 3: I made an honest inventory of the skills and knowledge I currently possessed and considered how I could apply them to my big goal. In other words, I recognized that I wasn't starting from zero.

Selling skills? Check. They would certainly give me a leg up when it came to finding and closing speaking opportunities. Presentation skills? Check. My experience with customers had taught me how to distill complex ideas and information into a compelling message, and how to connect them to the needs and wants of an audience. Subject-matter expertise? Check. I'd been selling for a decade, and I could speak credibly to the challenges that other salespeople faced.

STEP 4: I next made an inventory of what else I would need to succeed in this new career. For example, I needed a body of knowledge, something more substantial than war stories and lessons learned from my own experience. And I needed a brand behind me. Eventually my goal was to be my own brand, but at that point, nobody knew who Paul Cherry was. I needed a credential to give people confidence.

Here's what this exercise allows you to do: It allows you to paint a clear picture of where you want to be and chart a clear path for getting there. And that allows you to evaluate opportunities not only in terms of what they offer in the near term, but whether they move you forward to your ultimate goal.

Let me offer an example to demonstrate the principle. As I was thinking about how to reach my own big dream, I learned that Dale Carnegie was hiring salespeople.

If I hadn't gone through the exercise of setting a big goal and identifying what would help me get there, that probably wasn't an opportunity I would have pursued. It might have seemed to be an intriguing sales job and not much more. And if I were only thinking about the short term, it looked like a step backward. It was 100 percent commission. It offered no preexisting customer base. No flow of prequalified leads.

In fact, I did go backward at first. I made $19,000 my first year—not much for a sales job, even back then, and a serious pay cut from what I'd been making.

I gave up my comfortable sales job because the inventory I'd done helped me see it was actually a step *toward* my goal. They put me through intensive training (body of knowledge, check). I became certified as a Dale Carnegie instructor (powerful brand, check). I was given an exclusive territory and the opportunity to learn how to sell to the market.

Over the next few years, with a lot of hard work, I helped build a successful franchise for my boss. I was moving in the right direction. But now it was time to take stock once again.

Selling public workshops—thirty seats at $1,200 each—took most of my time and energy. There wasn't much repeat business, so I was continually refilling the bucket from scratch. And there were only so many hours in a day. Realistically, I was nearly maxed out.

I could continue to do what I was doing, and stay stuck where I was, or try to move forward.

Again, it was a risk. But my experience at Dale Carnegie, for which I'll always be grateful, equipped me with the knowledge and skills I needed to take the next step.

I thought hard about what that step would involve. What I really wanted was what had attracted me to the industry in the first place. I went through my goal-setting exercise again. It was the same dream, but now I could bring it into sharper focus. I wanted to sell six-figure contracts. I wanted to sell to businesses, not individuals. I wanted repeat business. I didn't want to be confined to a territory with a 120-mile radius. I wanted to do business wherever I wanted, across the globe.

Most of all, I wanted to carve out my own niche, to be a recognized authority in my own right.

In my sales career, I'd become deeply interested in the dynamics of questions. I'd learned that there really wasn't much I could tell customers to persuade them to buy. Customers have to sell themselves. And I'd noticed how asking just the right question, at just the right time, had a powerful effect on buyers. Socrates had discovered that secret thousands of years ago: A question is the world's most powerful tool to open someone's mind.

So I decided to make myself an authority on question-based selling. I sought out experts in the field. I talked to countless salespeople about the questions they asked. I thought about how I'd used questions in my own selling efforts and tried out new approaches to see how my customers would respond.

FAILING FORWARD

•

At the same time, I sought out a sales training company that would allow me to develop and apply these concepts. I found one that was excited about offering a fresh approach to selling.

In my first year with the new company, I won six-figure contracts with three major pharmaceutical and chemical companies. With a major brand behind me and a fresh approach to training, doors were opening up. We sold a major contract to a Fortune 100 company. We had professional trainers in the company, but my boss said: "You sold the training. You should deliver it." I had only two weeks to prepare, but I threw myself into it.

The big day came—and I bombed.

People weren't even nice about it. (There's one thing salespeople will not forgive you for: wasting their time. In sales, time is money.) They were laughing during the training, and not because I was trying to be funny. I actually heard the word "loser." I was not invited back.

That hurt bad. I was humiliated. I'd let down my client. I'd let down my boss. Did I want to give up? You bet.

Here's the only thing that got me through: dreaming big. I reflected on how far I'd come and how much I'd learned since my product-selling days. Yes, I'd pushed myself too fast and too far beyond the limits of my knowledge and expertise, and I'd fallen flat. I couldn't go back now, even if I'd wanted to.

That's an example of failing forward. By failing, I learned exactly what I needed to do to succeed. It showed me where my gaps were.

The dream was still there. Even more, I'd learned that the opportunity was real. Companies had shown they were willing to buy into the ideas I'd been selling them. Now I needed to learn how to deliver.

So, what about you?

What's your big dream? How can you leverage your knowledge and skills to get you closer to it? What else do you need to reach it? How will you acquire those skills, knowledge, and access? Are you willing to risk failure and learn from it? Or are you content to stay in your comfort zone, even if means trading away your dreams?

It's your decision.

2

KNOW YOUR WHY

Salespeople often focus on the how: "How do I get a customer to say yes?" "How do I counter an objection?" "How do I cultivate deeper relationships with buyers?" "How do I increase my sales?"

Take time to consider a different question: "Why?"

Sales is not an easy profession, so why pursue it?

According to common stereotypes, the answer is a no-brainer: to make a buck. In popular culture, salespeople are seen as simple creatures motivated only by the almighty dollar.

I'm not buying it. Yes, you can earn a good living in sales. But there are easier ways to make money.

I believe that the best salespeople find a deeper meaning in what they do. They enjoy the thrill of the hunt. They like to solve problems. They're energized by the idea of making things happen for their customers, their companies, and themselves.

I challenge you to have a conversation with yourself and discover what truly motivates you to do what you do.

To help facilitate that conversation, here's a look at how my own thinking about sales evolved:

As a young man, I never saw myself having a career in sales. I explored a variety of careers: I was accepted into flight school for both the Air Force and the Navy (but declined). I earned a master's degree in public policy and served in government for a short time. I had some jobs I hated. I even worked as a gravedigger (a job I actually liked). In this chapter, I will show my journey—including successes and failures—and why sales was the one thing I kept coming back to.

So what is it about sales that attracts me and keeps me motivated every day?

I have two answers:

1. It's a profession that always challenges you to do your best. We all know the old adage, "There's no second place in sales." Even when I win, I'm always looking for ways to be a little better next time. There's always something higher to aim for.

2. It's one of the few professions where you are ultimately accountable to yourself. Whether you work for yourself (as I do now) or for a larger organization (as I have in the past), sales comes with an objective scorecard. Either you're winning or you aren't. If you can sell—if you can put those wins on the board—you are rewarded not only financially, but also with autonomy and personal power. More

than in any other profession, I believe, selling gives people the opportunity to take charge of their destiny and create the life they want.

That's my why. But what about you? Do you truly understand why you found your way to a career in sales? And why you're now reading a book to help you get even better? It's true that people often get started on a path through a certain amount of serendipity: A certain job opened up at a certain time; experience in one industry leads to other opportunities in the same industry, and so on. But there's also a purpose. Some jobs don't fit, and people bounce out of them fairly quickly. We all know plenty of people who worked in sales and ultimately moved on to some other career path. (I don't consider these people failures, by the way; they had the courage to know what wasn't working for them and to find something better.) But if you've stuck with sales this long, there must be a reason why.

It's critically important to know what that why is. You don't have to tell anyone else, but get real with yourself. Your "why" is your compass. It keeps you moving in the right direction, especially when the path isn't clear. If you know that your why is the thrill of the hunt, for example, you won't make the mistake of taking a "farming" job servicing large accounts. It may be a great opportunity—for someone. But if it doesn't feed your why, you'll end up regretting it.

Knowing your why isn't as easy as it sounds. It requires deep reflection and honesty. So take some time—sit alone in a dark room if you must—to truly consider the question. And revisit the question regularly, because your why can change as your career evolves.

3

FIND THE RIGHT TRIBE

Here's a situation I've encountered over and over again: A young salesperson who's enjoyed some success has an opportunity to move to a different company or even a different industry. The potential upside is high and the risks seem low. After all, the salesperson has already demonstrated that he or she knows how to sell. Sure, there will be a learning curve because there's a different product and different customers, but at the end of the day, sales is sales.

If you've ever seen someone make this leap, or done so yourself, you know how the story usually ends. The salesperson fails at the new job, or at the very least struggles more than he or she expected.

What's surprising is that the problem is almost never the product or the customers. It's the organization—specifically, the fit between the salesperson and the organization.

Sales is a social enterprise. Most salespeople are part of an organization. Even those who work for themselves are part of a larger ecosystem, defined by the industry they serve, the niche they occupy, the territory they cover, and so on. Solo entrepreneurs and independents belong to tribes, too: industries and markets. They are webs of relationships, with hierarchies and rules you must master.

Your success as a salesperson depends on belonging to the right "tribe." In many cases, the right tribe depends on where you are in your career. Imagine, for example, that you have a few years of experience in software sales, and you have a customer who's about to join a hot new startup company. She's got funding, a great product concept, and crackerjack developers. She thinks you're awesome and wants you to come on board as their first salesperson. She's talking stock options, double-digit growth, perhaps the chance to be a millionaire in a few years. Hard to say no, right?

But here's the question you need to ask yourself: "Is this a tribe that can help me grow and succeed?" Are you at a point in your career where you need to tap into the wisdom and experience of veteran salespeople and sales managers? Do you have the skills, knowledge, and confidence to hold your own with prospects who are Silicon Valley superstars? Will the venture capitalists who are funding the startup give you the space to try, fail, learn, and try again, or will they need to see immediate results? And are you at a place in your career where you can afford to fail? In the long run, your best opportunity may be to spend more time with a larger and more stable organization, where you can master your craft. The startup company, on the other hand, may be the perfect tribe for someone else with the right combination of personality, experience, and tolerance for risk. It's all about the fit.

It may cost you more than you realize to move to a different company or industry and fail. When you change tribes, you abandon many of the relationships, internal and external, that come with membership in that tribe. (Research shows, for example, that salespeople who stay within an industry tend to be more successful than those who change industries.)

That's not to say you should never change jobs. It may be the only way to grow. But weigh the opportunities against what you give up. You have to rebuild those relationships. Or find a way to achieve both—that is, change jobs but maintain the relationships you already have.

All that being said, however, there are times when it makes sense to join a different tribe. When I joined Dale Carnegie, for example, it was definitely the right tribe for me. I gained enormous value from my time there. And then at some point it stopped being the right tribe. Not because it was a bad place or had let me down in some way. But my boss, who was a great guy and very supportive, told me one Friday afternoon that there was little if anything more he could teach me on selling. In fact, he said, he was learning how to improve his own sales skills by observing me. What a generous compliment—as I said, he was a great guy. But there was more I needed to learn, so it was time to move on to another tribe.

As you grow, start thinking about long-term fit. It's different for everyone. Some people are highly successful at inside phone sales. Some are born for field sales. Some people are really good at long-term, big-ticket, complex sales; they enjoy getting inside a customer's business and figuring out how to add value. Some are really good at getting people excited about products that others would consider simple, ordinary, or boring. Some are happiest working with individuals. Some sell with logic; some sell with emotion.

Think about what you're good at, what you want to be good at, what you aspire to. I know of a highly educated independent rep, an engineer, who sold relatively simple industrial parts such as springs and switches. He had a hugely successful and enjoyable business. He understood engineers and spoke their language. He got them, and they got him. Customers counted on him to find hard-to-source components, suggest alternative approaches, and help solve their problems. His "tribe" wasn't an individual company—none of them had a broad enough product line to allow him do what he did best. His tribe was his customers. He probably wouldn't have been successful within a company.

Another's passion was selling marketing programs. He was a highly creative person who'd started out in advertising. He tried the freelance route but was miserable. As an individual, he simply didn't have enough "inventory" to execute his great ideas. He needed to have an organization behind him. But it had to be the right organization, one that shared his vision of client service and willingness to take creative risks.

You can never be better than the organization you sell for. I know of a really smart rep who took a job with a company that had a lousy sales model. They were selling a complex service to a relatively unsophisticated audience (small-business owners). The service required a lot of explanation and hand-holding to be successful, but that was impossible given the sales volume required. As a result, the company experienced a high churn rate and low customer satisfaction. The rep was trying to service dozens of accounts every month, which didn't leave him enough time to provide the consultative service that his customers needed. He was in the wrong tribe. When he took his next job, he was highly focused on whether the pricing and volume could allow him to provide the service his customers needed for success.

Of course, you can't blame the tribe for your lack of success. Ultimately, your success or failure belongs to you and you alone. At the same time, if you're struggling, don't automatically assume it's because you're bad at sales (especially if you've had success in the past). Take a good hard look at your tribe: Is it one where most people can succeed? Is it one that aligns with your strengths as a salesperson? And is it one that aligns with your values? Unless the answer to all three questions is yes, you may need to consider finding a new one.

4

BE THE TOUGHEST BOSS
YOU EVER HAD

Here's another failing forward story from my career. I have lots of them.

The company I was selling for went belly-up. The economy was bad and sales jobs were hard to find. (Why do companies always seem to cut sales jobs when they're losing revenue? That's when they should be hiring *more*.)

After three months, I landed an inside sales job. It was not the job I wanted. I was overqualified. I'd been a top performer and now I was spending all day chasing nickel-and-dime deals. To be honest, I felt it was beneath me. But I had to pay the bills and told myself I could put up with it until something better came along. In the meantime, I assumed my superior sales skills would allow me to coast through this job without much stress and keep money coming in until I found something I really wanted.

Wrong. It turns out it's tougher to be a mediocre salesperson than a successful one. When you don't have the big wins to get you energized, the job gets harder and harder. And when you're in a sales job you hate, buyers pick up on it. They start wondering why they should do business with someone who's going through the motions. Every bad sales call makes the next one that much harder. Soon you're avoiding prospects and spending your day thinking about how badly you want out.

But there's nowhere to hide in sales, and before long my manager was on my back, telling me I wasn't pulling my weight and maybe wasn't really cut out for sales.

He believed in managing through fear and humiliation. We had to record our calls so he could listen to them and give us feedback. At one of our weekly sales meetings, he announced to everyone that he was going to demonstrate what *not* to do on a sales call. The next thing I heard was my own voice coming through a speaker. Minute after excruciating minute, I had to listen to myself botching the call while twenty of my peers laughed and hooted. These were the salespeople who were beneath me, remember?

Well, I knew I was done. The only question was when and how I'd be leaving.

But once I accepted that reality, an odd thing happened. I was liberated. I was furious at my boss for humiliating me. And I'll admit that I wanted some small measure of revenge. For me, that meant leaving on my own terms. *I* wanted to be the one to decide whether I would go or stay.

At our next one-on-one meeting, I took control. I told my boss that I would double my sales in the next thirty days or fire myself.

He was caught off guard. After all, it's usually the boss who gives the ultimatum. I made it clear that I wasn't going to beg for my job. And I wasn't saying this just to buy time. I was dead serious. Either I'd hit the goal or I'd be gone.

For the next thirty days, I was a selling machine. On every inbound and outbound call, I told myself, I was going to sell with purpose. The phone would ring. I'd take a deep breath, hold it for three seconds, and answer the call enthusiastically. I took charge of my pipeline. I stopped allowing prospects to put me off with excuses and delays. I called every pending quote and told the buyer it was time to make a decision. I spoke with confidence and authority.

Man, did it work. Sales were coming in, and after thirty days, I'd achieved the impossible. I had actually doubled my sales.

Soon after, I got another offer, and I quit that job. Maybe my boss felt bad, but probably not. No matter. I'd done what I'd done to prove something to myself. And I'd succeeded.

SET YOUR OWN BAR

Here's what that experience taught me: Be the toughest boss you ever had. My sales manager never could have gotten those results out of me. There was no combination of fear, intimidation, humiliation, or incentives that he could have used to motivate me to double my numbers. But when I announced that goal to him, I effectively fired him as my boss and replaced him with myself. From that moment on, I was working for myself, not for the company. And if I were going to be able to look myself in the mirror every morning, I'd have to do better. No more excuses. No more feeling sorry for myself. No more resenting my small-potatoes product line and small-minded bosses. None of that mattered, because I didn't work for them anymore. I worked for myself.

What about you? For whom do you work? Who holds you accountable?

Don't be content to meet the expectations of your boss or your company. Set your own bar, and set it high. You will work a lot harder to meet your *own* standards and expectations than anyone else's. Set your own goals and commit to the actions you'll need to take on a daily, weekly, and monthly basis to get there.

You don't have to go as far as I did. You don't have to publicly promise to fire yourself if you miss your goals. In fact, nobody needs to know your accountabilities except you. That said, you need to do what any good boss would do: Set measurable goals. Write them down. Track your progress. Have an ongoing, honest dialogue with yourself.

Why wait for your company to give you a pat on the back when you can do it yourself? Nobody knows what motivates you more than you do. Reward yourself when you perform well. Withhold rewards when you fall short. For example, if you hit your numbers for the month, celebrate by doing something that gives you pleasure—going out to dinner with the family, taking an overnight trip, buying new clothes. If you don't hit your numbers, tell yourself that you'll work even harder next month to claim the prize.

When you take charge of your own results, you'll most likely exceed any expectations set by your boss or company. They may congratulate themselves on what a good job they're doing managing your performance and keeping you motivated. Let them believe it. You know better. As an Ultimate Sales Professional, you've taken charge.

5

JUST MAKE THE CALL

My dad was in sales for forty years. He had his own business and inspired me to get into sales.

Whenever we got together, he'd always ask me the same set of questions:

"Where are you going this week?"

I'd tell him, "I'm going to Phoenix to run a training session."

He'd ask, "What are you going to teach them?"

I'd say, "I'm going to teach them how to sell."

"How are you going to do that?" he'd ask.

I'd be tired after a long day. I'd rather talk about something other than work. But he'd ask, and I'd try to tell him as briefly as I could.

One time when he asked me those questions, I explained I would be with one client for two or three days.

"What are you going to teach them?"

"I'm going to teach them how to sell."

"How are you going to do that?"

This time my guard was down. If I explained in detail, I thought, maybe he'd stop asking. So I started taking him through my sales process: the importance of planning, gaining rapport, asking good questions, presenting value . . ."

My father gave me a bewildered look. About forty-five seconds into my explanation, he said, "Why don't you just tell him to shake their ass and make the calls?"

I was taken aback. And then I start laughing. I said, "Dad, you're probably right. That's what they need to do. But if I tell them that, what am I going to talk about for the rest of the time I'm with them?"

GET IT DONE

•

Obviously, I believe there's a lot more to sales than picking up the phone. But my dad had a good point. All the techniques in the world don't count for squat unless you actually put them into practice.

Ordinary salespeople dream of a world where somebody else does the heavy lifting, where eager buyers are served up to them, just waiting to be closed. While they're dreaming, Ultimate Sales Pros are making calls. They know there are no shortcuts in sales. No magic bullets. No substitute for good old-fashioned hustle.

More than once, I've had clients where the salespeople don't need sales training. They just need to shake their asses and make the calls. Somehow, the client has allowed a culture to develop where lack of effort, procrastination, and excuses rule the day.

How many of us, including me, stare at the computer screen or the phone and let fear or anxiety stop us? We tell ourselves: "I'm not ready to make the call." "I don't know what I'm going to say." "I need to do more research." "I need to figure out what I'll say if the prospect says she needs to think about it, or she pushes back on price." "It's probably too early to call. Or too late." "She's probably not even in the office." "I already called him a week ago, and I don't want to seem desperate." The excuses we come up with! The precious selling time that's wasted!

These aren't issues of skill. They're issues of will. The solution is to just jump into the deep end and start swimming. It's like giving a presentation. Thirty seconds before you begin, you're thinking of all the things that could go wrong. You start talking, and in most cases you're fine. Once you stop worrying and start doing, all your training and preparation kick in.

So, take some advice from an old sales pro: Shake your ass and make the call.

6

THE POWER OF PROFILING

Most salespeople suffer from what I call *Prospect Anxiety*. They believe they can never have enough prospects. They believe that the number of sales they close—and therefore the amount of money they make—is directly related to the number of prospects they have.

Sales managers often perpetuate Prospect Anxiety by preaching the gospel of the sales funnel: To get one sale, you need to make x number of final presentations. To get the opportunity to make x number of final presentations, you have to qualify y number of suspects. To get y number of suspects, you have to talk to z number of prospects. However you do the math, the takeaway is the same: you need a huge and constant flow of leads into the top of the funnel to spit out a few sales at the bottom.

What happens when salespeople buy into this point of view? They believe that the reason they can't get more sales is because they don't have enough leads. They lean on their sales managers, who lean on Marketing to generate more leads. Marketing amps up the lead-generating engine and dumps a truckload of leads on the Sales Department, at which point salespeople complain that they're now buried in lousy leads. Like a picky eater, they toss aside the "bad" leads and continue to complain that they're still hungry.

Ultimate Sales Professionals have learned not to succumb to Prospect Anxiety. They don't worry about getting *more* leads. They're focused on getting the *right* leads. As a result, they maximize their most valuable resource: their time.

IT'S ABOUT EFFICIENCY

In sales, the limiting factor is almost always selling time, which means that *the only sustainable way to increase your sales is by increasing your efficiency.* And the problem with Prospect Anxiety is that it *decreases* your efficiency. You waste too much time with people who are unlikely to buy and too little time with your best prospects. So if you want to get more sales, get more efficient. Don't squander your time on non-buyers.

Does that mean that when your sales manager hands you a bunch of prospects to call, you toss them in the trash can? Of course not. Presumably they've gone through some sort of sifting process that makes them more qualified than a random person. Nor does it mean you should give up on prospects just because they're hard to reach. Your inability to reach a prospect tells you nothing about them. You can't properly qualify or disqualify a prospect until you've had some interaction with them. (Research shows, by the way, that you get the most sales when you make at least six follow-up attempts and that most salespeople make no more than one follow-up attempt, if that.)

What it *does* mean is that you qualify/disqualify prospects quickly, so that you don't waste any more time than necessary on low-probability prospects. And to make that assessment quickly, you must have a crystal-clear profile of what a high-probability, high-value prospect looks like.

Imagine, for example, that you have a prospecting list with one hundred names on it. Out of that one hundred, let's say twenty-five have a reasonable alignment with your profile. (Your information is limited, of course, so you'll have to make some reasonable guesses and fill in some blanks. But that's OK.)

You can't be sure these are qualified buyers. Nor can you be sure that people who don't fit the profile are duds. But prospects that align with your profile are *more likely* to be qualified buyers. So you're going to prioritize your prospecting efforts differently. You'll call the higher-probability prospects first. You'll pursue them more aggressively. You'll spend more time researching them. Assuming you have time, you'll still prospect the others, but you'll be careful not to overinvest in them. And you'll be quicker to disqualify them.

That means you'll be spending more time—and having richer conversations—with high-potential prospects.

True USPs take it a step further. They proactively *seek out* prospects who fit the profile. By finding your own prospects instead of passively waiting for leads, you increase both the quality *and* quantity of the opportunities available to you. You expand your pool of potential buyers while sifting out non-buyers.

Once again, the key issue is efficiency. The old idea of "dialing for dollars" will make a sales rep go broke fast. Some salespeople do the math this way: If it takes one hundred dials to make a sale, and a sale is worth $1,000, then each call is worth $10! But that's not true. Most of those calls are worthless. A few are worth a lot. If you can figure out which is which before you start dialing, so much the better. That's what customer profiling is all about.

PROFILING THE IDEAL CUSTOMER: IT STARTS WITH LISTENING

Some years ago, my client, a major insurance company, was facing an existential challenge.

Obamacare (formally known as the Patient Protection and Affordable Care Act of 2010) was just coming online, and it was going to fundamentally alter the way health insurance was bought and sold.

The insurance company sold through a huge network of independent brokers and agents. Traditionally, this had always been a highly intensive, consultative sales process. Brokers and agents added value to their clients by helping them navigate the ins and outs of the health insurance market, crafting highly individualized solutions tailored to their customers' needs. The insurance company, in turn, worked closely with the brokers and agents to support that effort. It was costly and time consuming, but the size of the deals justified the investment.

Obamacare was going to profoundly disrupt this business model. For one thing, by mandating certain coverage, it gave the brokers and agents a lot less flexibility in what they could offer their customers. At the same time, it created a marketplace where individuals and, to a certain extent, companies could go online and comparison shop different insurers' plans.

The net result was that sales were going to be a lot less consultative and a lot more transactional. And that meant radical disruption. My client, the insurance company, projected that of the ten thousand agents and brokers in its network, fully half of them would be out of business in a year.

Now, the insurer was still committed to providing the same high levels of support. In fact, it needed to work even more closely with agents and brokers to help them navigate this changing marketplace.

But it *didn't* want to overinvest in those who were going to be closing shop anyway. It wanted to focus its resources on its *best* customers—the ones most likely to succeed in the new environment. The problem was how to identify them.

We went out and started talking to brokers and agents. The more we listened, the more it became apparent that they fell into two camps: Some were already thinking hard about how they'd need to transform their business. They'd say things like, "We need to figure out how we'll get compensated for our expertise," or, "We need to become consultants." They didn't have all the answers, but they were focused on what they needed to do differently. The other group were like deer in the headlights. They had no plan. They were just waiting to see what would happen.

Seeing that distinction gave us a way to sort out the high-potential customers from the low-potential ones. We advised the insurance company's salespeople to ask brokers and agencies a simple question: "What are you doing to respond to the changes in the insurance marketplace?" The answers would tell our salespeople where to focus their time and attention.

If you're trying to find your best opportunities, talk to your customers. They will give you the answers, if you listen.

Here's another example:

A few years ago, I was working with a company called Frameco, which manufactures structural wall panels. It has great products, but it was getting nowhere. Contractors tend to be a conservative bunch. If they're used to putting up wood framing and it works for them, they're typically not interested in an alternative, no matter what advantages it offers.

The sales director started calling on customers they *had* won over. "Tell us why you bought from us," he asked. "What motivated you?"

One customer, a construction manager for a hotel chain, told him: "Simple. It's about time. With your system, we reduced construction time by 30 percent." He went on to explain what that meant in terms of money. "If you're building a hotel and can shave several months off the construction schedule, that means several more months of paying hotel guests." He did the math. It was a lot of money.

He had just profiled the ideal customer for Frameco. Not a stuck-in-old-ways contractor. Instead, someone who understood how much money could be made by accelerating a construction schedule—for example, construction managers for hotels, fast-food franchises, gas stations, apartments, and retail stores.

As a result of that conversation, he retargeted the prospect list and started calling on those people. And when he did, he knew exactly how to present his value proposition.

The customer had given him the answer. He listened. Over the next three years, Frameco increased its sales by a factor of five.

ARE YOU THE SALESPERSON YOUR IDEAL BUYER WANTS?

Profiling your ideal customers also provides guidance for your personal development. Imagine, for example, that you sell electronic components to a variety of industries, including consumer electronics, automotive engineering, medical devices, and telecommunications. You know something about all of these different industries, but you're not an expert on any of them.

Now imagine that your profiling exercise suggests that your best prospects are in the medical devices field. Do you have the specialized knowledge and skills you need to consistently win these opportunities? Do you understand what makes this market unique? Do you know where the industry as a whole is headed? Do you know the key players? What do your customers' customers care about? Do you know how the value proposition is different for these manufacturers versus, say, consumer electronics manufacturers? Which of your products are most relevant to their needs?

If you understand your best customers, you'll know what gaps you need to fill to be their best supplier.

Try to "own" that sector, and opportunities will start coming your way. If you're seen as the guru on medical devices, customers will refer others to you. People will know who you are. Your company will start feeding you those leads, since you're the one best equipped to close them.

FINDING THE RIGHT BUYERS:
A CASE STUDY

Here's an example of how profiling can transform your sales. This example involves an entire company, but the lessons apply equally to individual salespeople.

Arrowquip, a company that manufactures cattle-handling equipment, couldn't figure out why its sales were in the tank. Their products—what most people call "cattle chutes"—are used to corral one-ton bulls to administer medicine, work on their hooves, or brand them.

The company had a great reputation in their home country of Australia, where their products were known for safety, durability, and ease of use. They were more expensive than other cattle chutes, but the premium products more than paid for themselves. They allowed ranchers to handle more cattle in less time. Even more important, they required only one person to operate, where other cattle chutes needed two wranglers.

For the first three years, the company's sales strategy was to put its cattle chute on a trailer and haul it around cattle country in the United States and Canada. Just about every dealer they called on oohed and aahed. They agreed that these chutes really were different and better than others on the market.

But (there's always a "but") most dealers had reservations about taking on the line. They'd say, "Well, we've been selling Company X's cattle chutes for a long time, and we're pretty happy with how things are going."

The agricultural industry, like many industries, is cautious, conservative, and risk averse. Dealers weren't convinced that ranchers would pay a 30 percent premium compared with other equipment on the market. They already had long-standing relationships with other manufacturers, which they were reluctant to disrupt. And the company was asking dealers to make what looked like a risky bet: The dealers would have to submit payment up front for a truckload—anywhere from $35,000 to $45,000—and then hope they could move the inventory.

Despite the long-range road trips and dealers' enthusiasm for the product itself, the company wasn't making any progress in sales. So they turned to us for help.

The salespeople told us price was the problem, of course. Tightfisted cattle ranchers weren't willing to spend on quality, they said. When we looked deeper, however, a different picture emerged.

The real problem was that the company had absolutely no idea which dealers were good candidates to carry their products and which were a waste of time. To them, a dealer was a dealer. Dealers, they thought, all had the same needs and the same issues. So they all got the same sales pitch. The underlying assumption was that it was just a matter of chance which ones bought and which ones didn't. Obviously, the answer was simply to make more pitches to any dealer who was willing to listen and look at the equipment.

We asked the company to look at the accounts they had sold and identify the key attributes that set their best dealers apart. We found that their top accounts sold other premium product lines—which meant they had the experience, knowledge, confidence, and ability to sell value instead of price. We also looked at how much effort dealers put into providing exceptional customer service, and how much value they placed on that service. We looked at a variety of other factors as well, including product knowledge, their image and reputation, and the confidence and experience levels of their salespeople.

We worked up a profile of the types of dealers who would be good prospects for the company—for example, dealers with showrooms that were clean, organized, and well stocked, with lots of displays and a sales force that was comfortable selling premium products.

Once the company's salespeople knew what they were looking for, top prospects weren't hard to find. They'd get on Google maps and see what the dealer's storefront looked like and, often, what they had on their lots. They'd go to the dealer's website to see what brands they sold. They talked to high-end cattle ranchers and vets to find out which dealers they considered the best.

As a result, the salespeople weren't spending time trying to educate dealers who weren't focused on quality and were unlikely to buy. And because they were talking to the right dealers, they could focus their sales conversations on issues that mattered to them, such as quality and ease of use.

Not surprisingly, things clicked. Sales conversations were easy. These dealers understood value. They were progressive.

They were focused on growing their business, and they were curious. They didn't have to be "sold"; they immediately understood how these products would give them a competitive edge, expand their market, attract new customers, and offer new options to their existing customer base.

The proof of this strategy is in the result: By targeting the ideal dealer, the opportunity-to-close ratio went from 15 to 1 to 3 to 1. The company shortened the sales cycle and increased overall sales by a factor of four, not by putting more prospects *in* the sales funnel, but by taking prospects *out.*

The bottom line: Ultimate Sales Pros are focused. They zero in on what their ideal customers look like in terms of size, volume, customer base, years in business, credit worthiness, and so on. But there's more: They also look for intangible and subjective qualities—what marketing professionals call the "psychographic profile." Do the prospect's values, beliefs, and attributes align with what you're selling? If you sell for a company that is passionate about service, do they share that same passion? If your products are top of the line, do they care about quality? If you're looking for long-term relationships, how long have they been working with other vendors? When you know who your best prospects are and zero in on them, selling gets a lot easier and a lot more fun.

7

SALES FIRST, RELATIONSHIPS SECOND

I'm meeting with a sales manager at a company that makes orthopedic joint replacements. He's telling me how much pride his salespeople take in their relationships with surgeons.

It really is impressive. In medical sales, it's so difficult to win the respect of physicians, who tend to look at salespeople as an annoyance at best and hucksters at worst. And the days of winning over doctors with trips, tickets, and other freebies are long gone. What reason would a surgeon have to give a lowly salesperson even one minute of their astronomically expensive time?

Well, these salespeople had obviously figured out some reasons. With hard work over many years, they'd become not only trusted advisors but friends with the surgeons. They got invited to social functions, even family get-togethers.

Bravo. Well done.

"So," I ask the sales manager, "why are we meeting? Sounds like everything is going great."

A long pause. Then he says, "Well, I'm wondering whether these great relationships are costing us sales."

He goes on: "When I analyze the kind of business these salespeople are getting from their doctors, it's pretty much the same products over the years. There are many opportunities to upsell and cross-sell the other lines that we offer, but when I suggest this, the salespeople always resist. They say they don't want to come across as pushy or as taking advantage of their relationships. They say that if the doctors are interested in other things we offer, they'll ask."

I hear variations on this theme all the time: salespeople who use "relationships" as an excuse not to sell. One minute they're talking about how wonderful these relationships are, and the next minute they're telling you how it could all collapse in an instant if the salespeople had the gall to engage in, you know, actual selling.

Ultimate Sales Professionals understand that customer relationships are *business* relationships, and your business is sales.

I sincerely doubt that those surgeons harbored any illusions about the nature of the relationship. They know that salespeople have to make a living. And, guess what? *They don't have a problem with it.*

How do you know? Because they're already buying stuff! They like doing business with the salesperson. They value the products and find them useful. Why would these doctors be offended if the salesperson wanted to let them know about other products that might be useful as well? Upselling, cross-selling, and asking for more business aren't about being greedy or taking advantage. They're about helping the doctor better manage patient outcomes, increase compliance, be more profitable, and be a better doctor. If I were a doctor, I'd want to know.

If a customer is offended or put off by a salesperson doing his or her job, it's not much of a relationship to begin with. Good relationships allow you to take risks, like discussing other products that you sell. They allow you to ask tough questions and inquire about needs. Of course, you'd never push an unnecessary product or service on a customer. But if you can find a problem and you have a potential solution or want to explore other ways you can add value for them, why would the customer object?

Why assume that customers are so psychologically fragile? I think they understand the dynamics of a professional relationship even better than many salespeople. When I ask salespeople how they define a good relationship with customers, they use words like *trust, honesty, service, attention to the buyer's needs.* These are all wonderful and important elements of the relationship.

Yet, when I ask customers how *they* define relationships with their vendors and/or suppliers, I get a very different answer. Buyers are more specific, and their standards and expectations are much higher. They want more than to be treated well. They define a good relationship as one that delivers results, makes them profitable, reduces their risks, solves their problems, brings new ideas to stretch them, challenges them to grow, provides a competitive edge. On a personal level, they want a relationship that helps eliminate their stress, makes them look good, keeps them out of trouble, and more. They're not looking for a pal. They're looking for someone who can provide value.

See the difference? Most salespeople think of customer relationships in terms of pleasing and responding to the customer's needs. That's OK as far as it goes. But unless you are taking care of guests in a hotel or serving patrons in a restaurant, you're not really driving the relationship; you're just tagging along.

USPs, on the other hand, define their customer relationships the same way customers see them, and see nothing wrong with that. It's great to be friends with your customer, but both of you are really there to seek mutual advantage. In that sense, you *do* want to take advantage of the relationship. So does the customer. Both of you should profit from it.

Strong business relationships allow you to speak up when you see your customer is missing out, at risk, losing opportunities, working harder than necessary. You are there to help customers grow, give them an edge, eliminate or solve problems. Your customers may be the expert in what they do, but don't ask them to do your job. Don't expect them to be an expert in what you sell or to know which of your products and services they might need. You know more than anyone about what your products or services can do. You know what they've done for other customers, and how to make them work for this buyer. Your job is to take that knowledge, combine it with the customer's knowledge, and create value.

MORE THAN TRANSACTIONAL

•

Now, I'm not suggesting that you should have a strictly transactional relationship with customers, that it should only be about getting the order. You've got to work harder than that.

I had a salesperson in my sales training years ago who didn't like the way I was teaching questioning skills. He told me, "It all comes down to the same question: What can I do to earn your business?"

When asked at the right time, that can be an effective question. But usually it's a lazy question. In fact, when a salesperson asks *me* that question, I'm often at a loss about how to respond. How the heck should *I* know? It's basically saying to the customer: "I don't really want to spend any time getting to know you or to understand your needs. Can we just cut to the chase? Can I have your business?" What kind of message does that send to your contact that you want to cultivate a meaningful business relationship?

ASK FOR INTRODUCTIONS

•

Another area where I see average salespeople worry about "pushing" the relationship is when it comes to asking for introductions.

When I suggest that they cultivate relationships with others in their contact's organization, they push back.

I hear the same excuses. They don't want to step on their contact's toes, take advantage, or jeopardize the relationship.

If you have a great relationship with a customer, he or she will *want* to introduce you to others. Think of someone who's done good work for you—say, a good, honest mechanic. Aren't you eager to tell a friend who's looking for a mechanic? Do you hesitate even for a second?

No. "I know a great one," you say. "Honest. Prompt. Reliable. Really knows cars." Everyone wins—your friend, your mechanic, and not least of all, you—because you're the hero who hooked them up.

And imagine your mechanic came to you and said: "Look, I'm trying to expand my business. Could you tell your friends about me?" You'd be happy to, of course. You want your mechanic to be successful, for his sake and for yours.

So when average salespeople say that asking for an introduction would jeopardize their "wonderful" customer relationship, I have to wonder. Maybe the reason they don't want to ask is because, deep down, they know the relationship isn't as good as it could be. Maybe they don't really believe that they're adding value to customers. Or that the customer isn't really that loyal. If that's the case, work on the relationship. Work on your value proposition. But don't use the "relationship" as an excuse to do nothing.

GET REAL

•

In my work, I'm often asked to go out in the field with salespeople for coaching purposes. Many times, I'm brought in to help close the deal that's hit a wall. As the "new guy," the hope is that I'll learn something that the buyer hasn't shared with the salesperson.

It really makes no sense. How could I, with no relationship with the customer, find out more than the rep who's been cultivating this customer for months? What I often find out is that the salesperson *hasn't* built a relationship, because he or she is too worried about pleasing the customer. They're timid and obsequious. They haven't learned anything because they haven't asked tough questions. They haven't advanced the sale because, well, that might be pushy.

Is that the relationship they think the customer wants? Recommendations that are superficial or just plain wrong because the salesperson was afraid to ask questions? Do they think customers want to waste their time in meeting after meeting with no progress because the salesperson won't dare to ask what the holdup is?

Not long ago, I rode along with a sales rep who was trying to close a $500,000 opportunity for mining equipment. He'd been at it for eight months with no progress. Since I was new to the relationship, I started asking the buyer some questions about his background and how he got started in the company. He told me he'd started out in the sand pits making $10 an hour. Today, he's the only vice president on the leadership team who doesn't have a college degree and who worked his way up from the front lines. It's something he's very proud of. I also asked him about his goals for the year. He wanted to gain $4.5 million worth of additional business and maintain 34 percent margins. He knew how he was going to do it, and it was obvious that he took great pride in running a successful division. We talked about his long-term aspirations. He wanted to be the general manager for the entire mining operation.

And then he told us why the sale was stalled. It wasn't a state secret; nobody had asked him before. He was trying to close a contract worth $3 million, for which they would use our machine. I told him we really wanted to help him meet his income and margin goals this year. What could we do to help? Part of the issue, he said, was making sure parts and service would be available. We educated him on our service and parts availability.

We didn't close the sale that day, but perhaps we left him with a renewed sense of urgency to get his deal done, and a feeling that we were in his corner. Not long afterward, my client told me, the deal went through and the customer finalized the order.

A real relationship is based on honesty. Imagine your customer had a booger hanging from his or her nose as the two of you were about to meet his boss. Wouldn't you speak up? Or would that be impolite? If you're my vendor and we have a good relationship, I'd sure want you to say something. And if you didn't, I'd feel betrayed. In good relationships, we speak up. We ask questions. We get real.

8

DON'T GO NATIVE

For the most part, selling requires independence, resilience, motivation, and an entrepreneurial mind-set. But sometimes salespeople rely too much on themselves and not on all the other people in their organization. In fact, some salespeople see their own organization as the biggest obstacle standing between them and a successful sale.

Good salespeople are advocates for their customers. It's their job to marshal all the resources of their organization on behalf of their buyers. And not just because they believe in delivering great customer service. There's a selfish motive, too: They want the sale.

It's a good thing to stick up for your customer. It's a good thing to cut through organizational red tape or shake up a "we've always

THE ULTIMATE SALES PRO

done it this way" mentality to create more value. But there's a line, and Ultimate Sales Professionals understand it:

You don't work for your customer. And your objective is not to get the best deal possible for them.

Rather, your objective is to get the best deal for you *and* your customer.

Ask yourself: Would you expect your customers to sacrifice their best interests for you? For example, would you expect them to buy something they don't need just to help you make your quota this month? Would you expect them to worry about your company's profitability when they're negotiating a price? Of course not.

And do you think the customer holds you to a different standard? No.

Smart buyers will always ask for a better deal, and if you give them one they'll take it. But they will always assume (as they should) that whatever deal you're willing to agree to works for you and your company. You won't get any additional loyalty or gratitude. And in my experience, buyers who insist that you just need to do one more thing to win their business often don't come through for you in the end. Or they don't stick around long.

YOU NEED HELP FROM YOUR FRIENDS

•

In fact, when you "go native"—when you forget who you're working for and try to bully your organization into doing a deal at any cost—you do a disservice to your customer *and* yourself. For one thing, how committed is your organization going to be to a customer who's costing them money? How can they deliver outstanding value? How tempted will they be to cut corners? And do you really want to stake your reputation on that kind of relationship?

Even more important, when you browbeat your colleagues in the name of your customer, you undermine the very thing that will allow you to deliver the best possible value: your relationships within your own company.

Research shows that salespeople with strong internal networks get more sales than those with weak networks.

It makes sense when you think about it. If you need someone to go the extra mile for your customer—to expedite an order, for example, or waive a fee or approve a discount—you need to have a good relationship with the people who can make those things happen. You're more likely to get what you want if your own people trust you and believe you're on their side. Bullying or pestering may work in the short term, but it comes at a great, long-term cost. You'll do a better job marshaling the resources of your organization if you know your colleagues and understand what they do.

This way, you'll win the respect of buyers, too. Your service people will treat them better and sing your praises. And even if it means that sometimes you have to tell a customer, "No, we can't do that," you're in a position to explain why. Good customers will understand. Customers who aren't willing to find win-win solutions aren't worth the trouble. Cheapskate customers will bleed you dry with unrealistic demands. They'll suck up time that you could be spending with good prospects and customers. And eventually they'll kick you to the curb when they find a lower price.

Relationship selling means more than having good customer relationships. To be an Ultimate Sales Pro, one has to invest time and energy in internal relationships. It's not always easy. Conflicting priorities surface. People have hidden agendas. Your sales peers may feel competitive with you. Managers may set unrealistic goals. Bosses can be difficult and sometimes even incompetent.

The Ultimate Sales Professional rises to those challenges. He or she knows how to work the system to make it successful despite its flaws—how to persuade, cajole, inspire, praise, give credit, and negotiate when necessary.

Ultimate Sales Pros don't see themselves as lone wolves. They see themselves as partners with all of the people who are part of delivering great value to the customer. They show respect to others, give appreciation and recognition, and listen. And they seek it in return.

9

DON'T CALL ME— I'LL CALL YOU

I'm in Toronto on a ride-along with one of my client's salespeople. The client sells big equipment that crushes stone.

I'm watching the salesperson get crushed, and he doesn't even realize it.

The prospect certainly seems interested. He's impressed with the quality, performance, and ease of use of the particular machine that the rep is trying to sell. He shares with us that he's under a tight deadline to get the new equipment on board, because right now he's sourcing jobs out to subcontractors and it's costing him money. He casually mentions that he's got a new boss and just needs to get his approval before the go-ahead. As we wrap up the conversation, the prospect says: "I should know something by the middle of next week. Let's touch base then."

Promising? It sure sounds like it. It's a little concerning that this is the first time he's mentioned the need to get his boss to sign off. But it is what it is. There are times we just can't get in front of the top decision makers.

"Fantastic," the salesperson says.

I'm pretty sure I know what's going to happen next, because I've encountered this scenario countless times. The salesperson thinks he's a week away from a big sale. OK, two weeks at the outside. When he gets back to the office, he'll tell his manager three weeks, just to be on the safe side. The manager will add a week and plug that information into the forecast.

The following Wednesday, the salesperson will be waiting for the promised call. Thursday, he'll tell himself that the customer got busy, and will wait some more. Friday, he'll be wondering whether it's too soon to follow up, or whether the customer will be annoyed. Monday will do just as well for follow up, he concludes.

On Monday, he'll call and leave voice mail for the customer. On Tuesday, he'll send an email. The next day, a call and an email.

At some point, he'll finally get hold of the prospect, who will apologetically explain that they've been really busy and he hasn't had a chance to sit down with the boss yet. But by next week for sure . . .

Did you hear something? It's the sound of sales commissions slowly slipping away.

The truth is, most buyers are terrible at predicting when they are going to get back to us, or when they're going to make a decision. And the more time that goes by, the greater the chance you will lose the deal. If the customer isn't good at forecasting, how can the salesperson?

Ordinary salespeople fall into this trap over and over again. The customer says she'll make a decision in three weeks, or by the end of the year, or as soon as she has a chance to review the proposal. The salesperson puts a date into his projections. Throughout the company, other salespeople are also taking customers at their word. Is it any wonder that companies miss their sales targets by a mile? Or that every sales manager in the world is hearing the same story: How the deal that was absolutely going to happen in June now needs to be pushed into July (and at the end of July, into August, and on and on)?

But, says the earnest and hardworking salesperson, that was just a fluke. This time, the customer's word is rock solid. After all, why would they lie?

Well, for lots of reasons. But set that aside for the moment. Let's assume that the customer is absolutely sincere when she tells you the deal will close in three weeks. Here's the problem: Unlike you, her paycheck probably doesn't depend on getting the deal done. So despite her good intentions, it's easy enough to push back that decision. If other projects suddenly become more urgent, or the boss gets called out of town, or the money guys start getting nervous about cash flow, she can afford to wait.

MANAGE THE BUYING PROCESS

·

Of course, no salesperson, no matter how good, can force a customer to buy before he or she is ready. But in many, many cases, delays don't reflect an unwillingness to buy; they simply reflect a lack of attention and/or urgency on the part of the buyer.

That's why Ultimate Sales Professionals gather information that gives them a more realistic view of when the deal might actually close and what factors might delay it. Even more important, they use that information to *take control of the buying process.* They anticipate delays and help the buyer prepare for them. They ask things like, "What will you do if you can't get hold of your boss this week? Is that the only approval you need to get? Will you need to run it by the controller? What happens if the controller is on vacation? Will you have to keep outsourcing work until you get all the approvals in order? Remind me—how much is that costing you?"

The time to have these conversations, by the way, isn't after the customer has put you off. Have them early, when the customer is feeling that initial sense of urgency.

Here are the three most common mistakes that prolong the sales process, and the ways you can avoid them:

1. Agreeing to connect at some time in the future (next week, two weeks, a month) without setting a specific time and identifying what has to happen in that time. If the customer says, "I'll get back to you in a week," reply, "Sure. Can we schedule a follow-up at ten next Monday?"

2. Failing to test their sincerity. If customers really are interested in moving forward, they'll have no difficulty articulating the action steps that they'll be taking. You can be very direct. If buyers tell you they need a week, you might respond: "No problem. Can you walk me through what will happen between now and next week?"

3. Letting the customer/prospect agree to call you. That puts you in the position of waiting by the phone hoping they'll call. Don't let it happen. Tell the buyer: "Great. I'll call you on Monday at ten." As soon as you hang up, send an email to confirm. If the buyer persists, say: "I'll be busy with clients next week [or traveling, etc.] and hard to reach. So we can avoid phone tag, give me a good time I can call you."

If this approach strikes you as excessively pushy, your buyers probably see it differently. Consider the situation from their perspective. Even if they want what you're selling, buying is a chore. Presumably they want to get that chore off their plate sooner rather than later, and with as little fuss as possible. You're not trying to push them into a decision, but to clear away the obstacles that are bogging down the process.

Here's the distinction: A salesperson who lacks confidence will come across as pushy: "Um, when do you think you'll be able to talk to your boss and get back to me? By Tuesday? Wednesday? Because I can't guarantee that we'll be able to deliver by the first of the month unless we get a commitment this week." Buyers see through that in a millisecond. They can smell the desperation.

A confident salesperson, on the other hand, adds value by helping to manage the process. Their questions are designed to help the customer get what he or she already wants: "So if this looks like something you'd like to do, let's see how we can move this forward. Do you have access to your boss's calendar? Can you put a meeting on it for the three of us for Tuesday? Sure, while we're on the phone. I'll wait. . . . You set it up? Great. Now, what sorts of questions do you think your boss will have?

What additional documentation do you need to address those questions? I'll get it over to you this afternoon. OK, then, so your meeting with the boss is on Tuesday at two." By confidently guiding the customer through these steps, you've saved him a ton of time and administrative effort. Assuming he really is interested in your solution, he should be happy that the process is moving forward so quickly. And if he's not really that interested, if he's really just making excuses to string you along, isn't it better to find out sooner rather than later?

Obviously there's a fine line here. But buyers will let you know through their words or body language where that line is. And you may be surprised how eager the buyer is to let you take charge of the process. Everybody has too much to do, and it's one less thing they have to worry about. After all, you and your buyers are on the same side. The reason they engaged with you in the first place is because they had a need. Anything that helps them get to a solution sooner is in their interest as well as yours.

10

SELL SLOWER

I was working with a manufacturer of medical instruments that use lasers to measure blood flow. The products cost upwards of $50,000 and are sold primarily to medical research facilities.

With a niche product like this, the pool of potential customers is small, so you have to make the most of every opportunity. Unfortunately, the closing percentages for this company were low. That's why they brought us in.

We looked at the sales process. Typically, it would start with an email from a prospect, asking a question about price, availability, or some product feature.

The sales team was jumping on these opportunities, firing back an answer to the prospect's question, often within minutes, and then following up with a phone call. But these opportunities seemed to disappear as quickly as they appeared. Additional follow-up calls and emails mostly went ignored.

Understandably, the sales team was frustrated. Surely the prospect's first interaction with them had been all positive. The team couldn't have been more responsive or helpful. So why weren't prospects willing to take their calls afterwards?

The salespeople were right: They'd been unbelievably helpful. And that was the problem.

The prospects had gotten what they wanted. Which meant they now had no reason to talk to a salesperson.

SLOOOOOW DOWN

·

As I say elsewhere in this book, time is your most precious asset in sales. You need to use it wisely.

So it makes sense that salespeople should make full use of all the timesaving tools available in business today, right? You want to move things along as quickly as you can before prospects get distracted, lose interest, or find another vendor. Besides, buyers are busy, so you'll get bonus points for your responsiveness, right?

Well, not necessarily.

The problem with my client's sales force is that they were way too focused on efficiency. They thought they were doing the buyer and themselves a favor by trying to move the sale forward as quickly as possible.

But for big-ticket complex sales, *efficient* translates into *superficial*. Buying a $50,000 piece of specialized medical equipment is a big decision. Even if buyers are only in the "just looking" phase, there's a lot you need to understand before you can start to create value for the buyer. Why dash off a quick response without knowing anything about the buyer or the problem he or she is trying to solve?

Sales is like cooking. You can serve fast food at fast-food prices, but it's a tough way to make a living. If you want to serve a gourmet meal, however, it takes time to prepare it right.

With all the timesaving tools available to us—and all the pressure to close sales faster—the temptation to hurry through the sales process is almost irresistible. Email is so fast. And so seductive. You get an inquiry. You think about picking up the phone, but that takes time, and you might not get them. The reply button is sitting right there in front of you. The customer is waiting to hear from you. What could be easier?

Make them wait.

You're not Google. You're not in the business of dispensing free information to anyone who asks. Make buyers *earn* the right to the information they want from you. The price: a conversation. In other words, do *not* give new inbound prospects the information they ask for until you've had a chance to talk to them, one to one.

"But," you may object, "if I don't give it to them, someone else will!"

Maybe so. But remember, if the information the prospect wants is that easy to get, they wouldn't be contacting you in the first place. If they really need it, they'll talk to you. If they don't, well, they're just price shoppers and tire-kickers, and you shouldn't be wasting your time with them until they're serious about buying.

That's the approach I recommended to my client. The salespeople were understandably wary. But they were willing to give it a try. They agreed that, from now on, they would respond to these inquiries with a reply, thanking them for their interest and asking to schedule a conversation to better understand their needs and what they were trying to accomplish, and thereby make a suitable recommendation.

Guess what? In the vast majority of cases, the prospects readily agreed to a phone conversation.

The phone call basically went like this: "Thanks for your interest. So tell me about what's prompting your inquiry."

Inevitably, the prospect would describe their current research project and what they were hoping to do.

The salespeople would ask follow-up questions to get the prospect talking more: "Tell me more about this research. Tell me what instruments you're using now and why you're considering something else. Tell me, if you were to acquire our system, what would you use it for? How would it help your project?"

These conversations were easy. They were giving scientists and medical professionals a chance to go on and on about their programs and projects. For many prospects, the project was their baby. It was something they were very proud of. If successful, it would give them exposure, get them published, help patients. If it failed, it would be a blow to them and their institutions.

Once they got prospects talking, the salespeople could easily learn everything they needed to know to properly qualify the buyer and begin to craft a solution. They'd learn the buyer's timeline, where the funding would come from, who would be involved in the decision and any other needs the buyer might have.

By insisting on these conversations, the company more than doubled its sales. They were much more effective at identifying high-potential leads and weeding out tire-kickers. Perhaps most surprising, by slowing down the process they actually *shortened* their sales cycle, because they acquired so much information in that very first call.

The lesson for Ultimate Sales Professionals: Don't try to hurry along a sale. And don't give prospects a reason *not* to talk to you. Seek every opportunity to engage in in-depth conversations with buyers. That's absolutely the best use of your limited time.

11

MASTERING THE VALUE EQUATION

I don't worry when buyers say, "Gee, your price is kind of high." I could argue with them and point out that my prices are competitive for my industry. But why? If high prices were a deal breaker, Lamborghini would never sell a car.

Granted, not everyone can afford a Lamborghini. But affordability is a different issue and a different conversation. Other people *can* afford it but don't think it's worth the price. That's a perceived value problem, not a price problem. Again, a different conversation.

I empathize. High-quality training and consulting services *are* expensive. It takes a lot of time to do my job right: working with clients to understand their needs and problems, coming up with a solution tailored to their specific needs, delivering a program that gets salespeople engaged, following up. And my time is not cheap. Clients get the benefit of my experience with hundreds of other clients over the years.

I tell them that they can certainly find a lower-price option, and if that's what they really want, I'll happily send them on their way. But what I *won't* do is sell them a Lamborghini at a Chevy price.

I have a friend who spent many years working at advertising agencies. It's the same deal: Agencies are expensive. They hire talented people and have to pay them well to keep them. They have a lot of overhead. And sometimes prospects (usually unsophisticated ones) object. Why pay agency rates for copywriters and designers when there are plenty of hungry freelancers who would do the job for less?

Here's why: They get more value. When clients face a crisis or need a big project in a hurry, the agency can put as many of those highly talented people on it as necessary and manage the job to make sure it gets done right. When a client needs a new strategy, the agency taps into a staff of experienced marketing experts to chew on the problem. Unlike freelancers, agencies don't go on vacation or disappear in the middle of an assignment or drop the ball because they found a better gig. Expensive? Sure. You can't deliver that kind of value on a freelance budget.

Experience has taught me that most people don't want a cheap solution. They may take a shot and ask for a better price, but when I say no, few of them walk away. What most customers want—at least the ones I'm interested in working with—is *value*.

THE VALUE EQUATION

Sales guru Neil Rackham offers a deceptively simple definition of customer value, which is a powerful tool for Ultimate Sales Professionals:

Value = Benefits − Cost

Or

V = B − C

Simple as it is, the Value Equation helps you address price objections and shift the focus of a sales conversation. It's also a useful way for salespeople to think through their value propositions in general; to consider how various benefits might be evaluated by different customers, which ones to lead with, how to frame them. It also helps you think about how customers perceive cost (which is not the same as price). And it perfectly mirrors the thought process that customers use, consciously or unconsciously, to evaluate your proposal.

Working through the Value Equation with a customer is a foundational selling skill, and it's one I teach often. But to really elevate your practice, there are deeper levels to the equation, and when you master them you can be even more effective at creating high-value proposals that will help you outsell the competition and win more and bigger deals.

Let's use a real-world example (with some details changed to protect the guilty):

Smith runs a production facility that processes potatoes. Every week, several tons of potatoes arrive at the plant and are transformed into frozen French fries, curly fries, and other potato products.

LEVEL 1
VALUE VERSUS THE STATUS QUO

•

The most basic Value Equation is how you stack up against the status quo—what the customer is or isn't doing right now.

You call on Smith. You explain that your equipment can slice potatoes faster than the old equipment he's using.

"New slicers are expensive," Smith says. "I can't afford them."

You know what to say, of course. "You'll save money. Tell me how many potatoes you process every month and how much revenue they generate. I'll show you how much more money you can make with our faster potato processor."

Pretty simple, right? $V = B - C$. You deliver a benefit that more than offsets the price. Smith should be begging to buy from you. So are you walking away with an order?

No.

LEVEL 2
VALUE VERSUS THE COMPETITION

•

The Level 1 Value Equation got Smith interested. He sees the potential to make more money. But you're not the only potato-slicer seller in town. So now his focus shifts. It's no longer the value versus the status quo. It's how your value compares with competitors.

Salespeople can get tripped up at this stage, because they fail to recognize that the game has changed. They're still talking value versus the status quo while the customer is looking at comparative value.

Back to our example: Smith asks his purchasing agent to gather some proposals and find the best deal. Lou, the purchasing agent, draws up specs and solicits proposals from three companies:

- You quote a price of $205,000 for the new equipment and installation.
- Company X sends in a price of $230,000.
- Company Y has the lowest bid at $185,000.

Lou assumes that the machines in each proposal offer equivalent benefits. They all slice and dice. They all handle similar throughput.

Although Lou may not be thinking explicitly in terms of the Value Equation, he's doing the math the same way. If benefits are equal, the lowest cost yields the highest value. He awards the contract to Company Y.

Oops. Lou confused the purchase price with cost.

Three months later, Company Y's new potato slicer breaks. Smith calls Company Y, who says the technician can't get there for two days. Meanwhile, Smith's plant is completely shut down.

He didn't factor in the cost of downtime—how much money he's losing while he waits for Company Y to service his broken machine. Let's say his plant averages one thousand bags of potatoes each hour, and the bags sell for $2 apiece. This means he's losing $2,000 in revenue each hour. After forty-eight hours, that's $96,000 down the drain. Looking back, was it worth it to buy the cheapest equipment just to save $20,000 to $45,000?

Obviously not. Somebody should have warned him. Like you.

Good salespeople, especially those who sell higher-priced products, know how to have these conversations with customers. And sophisticated customers don't need much prodding to accept the logic that cost involves more than the purchase price. So you have to wonder why Lou, who presumably has a lot of experience with equipment, didn't know better.

Here's where it starts getting complicated. Lou *did* know the risks of downtime in a general, vague, theoretical way. But he didn't start doing the actual math until he was faced with the problem. And there are another whole bunch of elements to the "B" (Benefits") and "C" (Cost) factors that Lou hasn't even thought about. Not that he's stupid. But he's a busy guy trying to keep the line running. He doesn't have time to do the hard thinking.

USPs do the hard thinking. They're experts in *all* the factors that affect benefits and costs, giving them more ways to influence the Value Equation.

Knowing that customers are skeptical, they don't try to force their Value Equation on the customer. Instead, they frame a series of questions that help customers arrive at the right solution on their own.

Here's how that conversation might have gone with Lou:

"Lou, have you factored in reliability? Our equipment has the highest reliability in the industry, which is one reason it costs a little more. Let's see what that reliability might be worth to you: If something breaks, how long will it take to fix? We promise twenty-four hours. Did you check with other buyers to see what their experience with Company Y is? And what will that downtime cost you in terms of production? Let's do the math. . . ."

Here are some other ways you can do the hard thinking for Lou:

"Lou, if you need to expand capacity in the future, will you have to buy equipment all over again? Our equipment is modular, so you can expand capacity at a very modest cost." (Reduces potential cost down the road.)

"Lou, *Potato Chip Weekly* reports that consumer demand for waffle chips is growing like crazy. Our newest slicer also does waffle chips. Our competitors don't." (Potential to get into a growing sector of the market.)

"Lou, we offer a financing package that gives you a lower interest rate than most banks are offering." (Lower total cost of ownership.)

Each of your competitors will have their own Value Equation. Your customer will be evaluating the offers by totaling up all the benefits and costs for each of you and looking for the highest V. So of course, you need to maximize your benefits and minimize your costs.

Your competitors will be trying to do the same. So once you've honed your Value Equation, you need to consider their Value Equations as well. To tip the decision in your favor, look for ways to **discount** your competitor's **benefits** and **add** to their costs.

It's a delicate art, because you don't want to speak ill of your competitor. But you do want to give your buyer relevant, objective information so he or she can make an informed decision.

To be successful, you have to understand your competitors' Value Equations as well as you do your own. You need to know what they'll say or do to get the business. You have to know what benefits they'll lead with, and how you can discount them without trashing your rival. ("Company X makes great potato slicers. They have an impressive throughput rate in tests. But be sure to ask how the equipment performs in real-world conditions. Here's a third-party report on that.") You have to know what costs competitors are going to try to hide or soft-pedal and get the buyer to factor them in. ("Replacing the knives in slicers can get expensive. Our customers tell us that they save considerable money because our slicer knives don't have to be replaced as often and can be replaced without shutting down the entire production line.")

And you have to be right. You have to know the ins and outs of your competitors' products as if you're selling them yourself.

What's interesting about the Level 2 analysis is that you only have to be a little bit better than the competitors. At Level 1, when you're trying to move away from the status quo, you need to show a big upside, because people view *any* change as a cost. But when you get to Level 2, the buyer is already psychologically disposed to spend the money. You just need to be the best choice.

The worst way to try to add value, by the way, is with a lower price. Competitors can match a price cut. Buyers will play you against each other. You give away value and get nothing in return.

THE HIDDEN COMPETITOR

Even when you can offer more value than competitors, you're still not guaranteed to get the sale. There's another, hidden competitor that you have to consider: all the other things a customer could be spending the money on. Often the choice isn't between you and a competitor, or you and doing nothing. It's between you and something else that someone else in the organization wants to do with the same money.

This is where salespeople often get frustrated. The buyer is enthusiastic right up to the end, and then at the last minute he or she tells you that the sale got nixed by a higher-up. It's easy to feel that your buyer has been lying to you all along. But there's a very real possibility that the buyer was as surprised as you were. The buyer may not even know what happened; higher-ups may say only, "It's not in the budget."

You can't always anticipate who in the organization might be competing for those dollars or what they want to do with them. Your best defense is to really dig deep to understand how your customer makes and spends money. It's legitimate to ask your buyer (or someone higher up, possibly): "What are the company's top priorities right now? How's cash flow? Is there enough to fund everything the company wants to do, or will you have to fight for your budget? Who's in favor? Who's opposed?" These are tough questions to ask, and you may not get straight answers, but the more you learn, the better you'll be at crafting a successful Value Equation.

THE TRUST MULTIPLIER

•

There's one more factor that has a profound influence on how the buyer perceives value: whether they trust you. You can talk all day long about value, benefits, and cost, but if you lack credibility with the buyer, you may as well be talking to yourself. So we should modify the Value Equation to look like this:

$$V = (B - C) \times T$$

The trust multiplier is one of the most effective ways to beat the competition. Most vendors can present a competitive value proposition, or they'd soon be out of business. Some may emphasize certain benefits over others—one may promote ease of use while another stakes its claim on reliability, for example. So with any given buyer, one vendor may have an edge if its value proposition aligns more closely with what the buyer is seeking. But those differences pale in comparison to the trust multiplier. Am I going to buy the product that looks perfect on paper from a vendor I don't know or trust? Or will I choose a vendor I trust and work with them to make it work?

So don't overlook the importance of establishing that trust throughout the sales process. Third-party data, for example, can increase their trust in your analysis. Invite them to talk to your existing customers to validate your numbers. Acknowledge the costs or limitations of what you offer before your competitors point them out.

LEVEL 3
VALUE BEYOND MONEY
•

At the highest level, the V in the Value Equation involves more than money.

You want to frame your Value Equation in relation to the things that are most important to the organization and your individual buyer. If the most valuable thing is revenue growth (for example, to attract investors), talk revenue growth. If it's market share, talk market share. If it's cash flow, talk cash flow.

Let's say that our prospect, Smith, has been supplying potato chips to Jones Snack Foods for the past twenty-five years. Jones is Smith's biggest customer. Their parents did business together. When Smith's daughter got married, Jones was at the wedding. Their families go on vacation together. If you understand that relationship, you're going to know how to deliver the highest possible value to Smith. Let's say Jones is falling behind his competitors, and a new line of waffle chips would be just the thing to help him win back market share. If

Smith can help his old friend Jones (not to mention himself) by buying your waffle-chip potato slicer, is Smith going to say you're too expensive?

The deeper you go into what the organization values, the less the conversation will be about dollars and cents. You need to make a business case, of course. But when you get to the heart of it, the things that matter most are, literally, priceless. Quality. Integrity. Reputation. Reliability. Relationships. If you can frame your value proposition in a way that promotes the organization's deepest values, nobody's going to haggle over price.

12

CUT THROUGH THE CR*P

I recently accompanied a sales rep on a call. The rep's company manufactures air filters for the HVAC industry.

Most customers in this industry are straightforward. Either they buy air filters or they don't. If they do, they generally buy them from one of a handful of suppliers, for all the usual reasons: the right product, the right price, good technical support, availability, a long-standing relationship with the supplier, and so on. No big mystery.

We got a referral from a current customer, a vice president who loved how the filter designs enhanced productivity and reduced labor costs in his plant. He connected us with a service manager in another division within his company. It should have been an easy sale.

When we met, we exchanged pleasantries with the service manager. We asked some questions about his background and looked for common ground where we could start to connect our value proposition with his operation.

He wasn't going for any of it. It was pretty obvious that he'd agreed to the meeting only because the VP had asked him to. He gave noncommittal answers to our questions. "Sure," he said, "I'm always open to what else is out there." And, "If you can offer me a better price, I might consider it." As the meeting was concluding, he said, "Send me your price list."

What to do?

Price is not a relationship driver; it's a transactional driver. But shouldn't we at least do what he'd asked? It was a foot in the door, right? We could send it and then call back and see if he got it (which, of course, he would) and try to chat him up some more. But if all you get is a foot in the door, you usually end up with nothing more than stubbed toes.

Besides, price wasn't even a valid issue. If he really cared about price, he'd have asked us for one. He didn't even do that. He asked us to *send him a price list.*

There was something he wasn't telling us. Despite our questions and polite prodding, we couldn't get it out of him. To this day, I don't know what made this guy so resistant. But it was clear that he wasn't interested in reducing his labor costs or improving his productivity.

So did we agree to send the price list? Nah. It wasn't worth the stamp, or the time to lick it, or the effort to press the send button to email.

We made some noncommittal response and thanked him for his time.

DID YOU SMELL SOMETHING?

•

Prospects, of course, are under no obligation to be straight with you. They're free to give you whatever line of BS they choose.

But you're under no obligation to step in it.

We didn't. Instead, we sidestepped. We found someone else who cared about value in his organization. It turns out it was someone higher up. We set up a meeting.

Of course there was a chance that the service manager would get his nose out of joint if he found out we were going over his head. But really, what was the risk? What did we have to lose?

As it turned out, the higher-up loved what we presented. We got the sale. And if the service manager had a problem with it, we never heard about it.

GIVE IT TO ME STRAIGHT

•

Customers have many ways of yanking our chains, and many reasons to do so. They can use us to get some free advice by pretending to be interested in what we sell. They can try to get a price from us just to get a better deal from their existing supplier. They can demand outrageous terms and hope we're dumb enough to agree to them. They can pound the desk and raise their voice to try to wring out a concession and laugh about it as soon as we leave. They can give us a little bit of business just to keep us around in case their current vendor goes astray. They can promise us future business that never materializes. They can put us off, never make a decision, dance around issues, avoid confrontation, withhold critical buying information, or pursue a hidden agenda at our expense.

Over time, most salespeople develop a good nose for BS. They can tell the difference between a customer who's being straight and one who's not. They tell their colleagues, their bosses, their spouses: "Let me tell you about the line this guy was handing me today."

But what they *don't* do is confront it.

Ultimate Sales Pros do.

Most customers—especially in complex sales—buy because they value the relationship. So USPs zero in on their relationship with the customer. No relationship, no sale.

And if someone isn't being honest, what does that say about the relationship?

You can't build a good relationship without honesty. So if you're getting the runaround from a prospect, stop the conversation and call him on it. You have nothing to lose. If he's not telling you the truth, you're not likely to get his business anyway.

Don't be rude, of course. But be direct. Put on a big smile and say something like, "Anna, you're being very polite and I appreciate you trying not to hurt my feelings. But I feel we're not making much progress here. So I wonder what I'm missing."

Sometimes a question like that is all it takes for a buyer to get real. But not always. "Oh, no," the buyer might say. "I really *am* interested, but it's just that my boss is really busy, or budgets are tight," or so on.

To which you might reply: "I'm sure all those things are true, Anna. But in my experience, buyers who really want to move forward find ways to deal with those issues. So level with me: What else is holding you back?"

Does this approach always work? Of course not. Some buyers will never tip their hand. Maybe they see you as a threat to their job. Maybe they're giving their business to a friend. Maybe you didn't say hi to them in the elevator one day.

But sometimes—more often than you think—buyers will actually *answer your question*. I've seen it happen countless times. They're not used to dealing with salespeople who have the confidence to cut through the cr*p. They're taken aback at first. And then it dawns on them that maybe you're the kind of salesperson they want to deal with. You've given them permission to be a straight shooter: "Well, since you mentioned it, there is *one* thing. . . ."

Now you're on your way to building a relationship that can result in a sale.

"CALL ME NEXT MONTH"

•

Here's a real-life example:

Terry was new at selling construction equipment. He'd been at it for about a year. He kept getting the brushoff from prospects: "I'm too busy. Call me back in a month."

Terry knew he was getting a line of BS. But what could he do about it?

We talked about what he could do. We practiced how to confront the situation in a polite but firm way.

The next time a prospect told him, "Call me back in a month," here's what Terry said: "Tom, I'll be happy to get back to you next month. But help me out here. When I call you in a month, what exactly are we going to be talking about? The reason I ask is because we've been going back and forth on this for the past twelve months. So where exactly do we stand on this?"

A long pause. Finally, the prospect said: "Fair enough. I guess we're going to talk about what you can do for us."

Terry wasn't done. "Tom, that sounds great," he said. "But the fact is, we could do a lot of things for you. It really depends on what's most important to you. So let me ask you: What issues matter most to you?"

Next thing Terry knew, the prospect launched into a monologue about the challenges he was facing and what he was trying to achieve. In other words, he was revealing exactly how Terry should sell to him.

Fifteen minutes of honesty versus twelve months of BS. Which was more valuable?

QUESTIONS THAT CUT THROUGH THE CR*P

•

Here are some other questions you can ask to encourage your prospect to get real with you:

- What is it I am failing to understand about what's most important to you and your company?

- Help me see what I'm not grasping, so I can help you achieve your goals.
- There's something else going on. What is it?
- I understand you're too busy to talk right now. And I don't want to waste your time scheduling a follow-up call if this is unlikely to be a good fit for you. May I ask a couple of quick questions to see if we have a reason to schedule a call?
- I understand you have to discuss this with your boss. So how do you think he or she will react? And what's your level of commitment to go to bat for this?

Do you see a common thread in these questions? They're confident. What you sell is valuable. You don't have time to waste. You have every right to expect straight answers and not a runaround.

By contrast, when salespeople use phrases like, "Can I stop by?" or, "Would it be OK if I talked to your boss?" or, "Would you mind if . . . ?" they're begging. And begging implies that they have nothing of value to offer.

The USP speaks with authority—authority based on the value you're prepared to deliver. USPs never beg; they *assume the next step*. They say, "Let's do this," or, "I recommend that the next step would be . . ." or, "I suggest we go forward in this way. . . ." They project confidence because they know they have something great to offer. They don't put the prospect on a pedestal; they see the buyer as an equal—a partner and ally in a mutually advantageous relationship.

13

SELL WHERE
THE BUCK STOPS

When I first started in sales—selling Yellow Pages advertising—90 percent of my customers were small-business owners,
so I learned the value of talking to the person where the buck
stopped. For the most part, the business owner made the buying
decision. Sure, there were times when he or she had to talk to a
spouse, mom, dad, or partner, but in most cases I was talking to
the person who was going to make the call. What a wonderfully
efficient way to sell.

Of course, as I moved into selling big-ticket items to larger
organizations, things got a lot more complicated. There was
seldom a single decision maker. You had lots of wannabes—
people who insisted that they had the power to do the deal
(and often believed it themselves), when it turned out they

were just the screener. You had people who could say no and kill the sale but couldn't actually say yes. You had actual decision makers who liked to lurk in the background and then emerge at the very end, forcing you to start the sales process again from scratch. You had people who said they were interested but never intended to buy from you and were only using you to get a better deal from the people they really wanted to do business with. You had people who would pretend to be buying, when all they really wanted was free consulting. You had organizations where people weren't even sure who could do a deal and who couldn't. As I'd search for someone, anyone, who could sign off on a deal, I sometimes felt like that Greek philosopher Diogenes—you know, the guy carrying the lantern as he looked for an honest man.

According to Wikipedia, Diogenes was one of the founders of the Cynic school of philosophy. When it comes to finding a real decision maker, call me a disciple.

Even so, I found one rule carried over from my Yellow Pages days: When you could actually find a person where the buck stopped, it was much simpler to sell. Not necessarily easier, but simpler. You weren't dealing with all the internal politics, posterior protection, puffery, and gamesmanship that go on in the middle ranks of big organizations. People who *are* important don't need to *feel* important. They're more concerned with what you sell and whether it can help them get the things done that they want or need to get done. Are they tough customers? You bet, but at least they really *are* customers. Will they chew you up and spit you out if you're not prepared? Yes, but if you can demonstrate and deliver value, they will get the deal done. They make things happen. That's how they got to be in charge.

So it astonishes me that so many salespeople seem to prefer calling on people who can't, won't, or are afraid to make a decision.

One of my clients sold medical equipment supplies to hospitals. The vice president of sales constantly hammered this message to his salespeople: Sell up. Call on the senior-level hospital executives, folks who care about important issues like growth, profitability, competitiveness, patient outcomes, safety, and so on. These people are grappling with big challenges, which mean big opportunities for sales.

Yet the salespeople would always gravitate to the bottom, calling on materials managers (essentially purchasing agents). These prospects weren't dealing with big problems. Their job was to deal with only one problem: price. So they got really good at squeezing salespeople on price and had little or no interest in discussing value.

Why were the salespeople wasting their time with these low-level price grinders, especially when their boss was telling them to aim higher?

Well, a few reasons.

First, it was fairly easy to call on these contacts and get an appointment. The materials managers were happy to talk to salespeople. The more salespeople they talked to, the more they could price shop and the more they could play one against the other.

Second, low-level buyers tend to focus on features and benefits: "What do I get for my money?" Salespeople can talk features and benefits in their sleep. They'd give their spiel; the materials manager would ask, "How much?" The rep would give a number, and then in a low voice add: "But if you order this much, I can get you a discount." It doesn't require much skill or effort.

And third, unsophisticated salespeople tend to confuse the person whose signature is on the purchase order with the decision maker. The two are not the same. But this way they could go back to the boss and insist that they're having great conversations with a buyer at Hospital X, and there's a really good chance they'll buy something.

RAISE YOUR SIGHTS

•

Calling on higher-level executives, on the other hand, is hard work. It's difficult to get an appointment. And if you do get one, you have to prepare more and think harder. If you launch into a standard features-and-benefits pitch, the busy exec is going to shuffle you back downstairs to meet with the materials managers or purchasing agents. So you've got to do your homework and have a sophisticated understanding of the buyer's world. You've got to have good answers to tough questions.

Why work that hard?

Because you get bigger and more profitable deals. Because you're not stuck in bidding wars with lowball competitors. Because when you can demonstrate a real impact on things that matter to the organization, you're going to get invited back and offered more opportunities.

Here's an example of how Ultimate Sales Pros sell to high-level decision makers:

Imagine you're selling deli meats and related products to supermarkets. It's a basic commodity sale, right? Hot dogs. Sliced turkey. You go into stores and talk to deli counter managers. You offer samples. If they like your product, they might order some stuff from you—if you can cut your price.

Nothing there that would interest the higher-ups, right?

That's how most suppliers approach the business. But I learned about one that took a different approach.

When their reps called on a new account, they didn't start with the deli manager. They didn't bring samples. They called on the C suites of major food store chains.

They got appointments because they made it clear that they weren't there to talk about products or price. They wanted to talk about how they could help the supermarket chains expand market share, improve profitability and sales volume, and reduce overhead. They proposed coming into the stores and running the entire deli operation, selling their own products and competitors' products as well. They would leverage their expertise and knowledge—which, when it came to deli counters, was far more extensive than that of the chains—to provide a turnkey, outsourced solution that would add more money to the bottom line.

Using this approach, this supplier captured a significant share of the premium deli products market.

Those are the kinds of conversations that top salespeople have. And if you don't think you can bring that sort of thinking to your customers, I would submit that you're not thinking hard enough. It's not brain surgery. But you have to do your homework. You have to understand what drives your customers' business and think about how you can affect it.

Here's another example:

A client of mine, Arrow Specialties, sells promotional products—things like pens, notepads, T-shirts, jackets, key chains, so on and so on. You'd think it's a commodity business—lots of companies sell these kinds of items. Most have similar product lines and similar quality. Customers have lots of vendors to choose from, and often shop based on price and delivery.

Arrow is a family business, and the brothers who run the sales operation, Drew and Duane Mailey, have a unique perspective on the market. It's not about selling T-shirts or trinkets; they're selling tools to help clients build their image, brand, and market reputation. For clients in the construction business, for example, it's about providing workers with name-brand, high-end work jackets, overalls, and safety clothing. It's a way for the construction company to send a message to the workers: We provide you with the best because we value what you do. The workers take pride in what they wear. Customers, passersby, and job applicants see how people are dressed, and that becomes an effective marketing and hiring tool as well.

One of Arrow's customers, a drilling company, was spending about $100,000 per year. That's a sizable account in this industry. Ordinary salespeople would have been thrilled and told themselves they were wringing as many sales as they could out of the company.

Drew and Duane saw a much larger opportunity based on the size of the company, perhaps as much as $1 million a year. But as things stood, the orders were strictly transactional. The human resources manager was ordering items online. She had no interest in meeting with a salesperson.

To win an opportunity of that size, they knew they had to go higher up the ladder; probably all the way to the CEO.

They called the CEO's executive assistant. "We want to thank him for all the business you've done with us over the years. We were hoping you could tell us what size shirt he wears and help us set up a time when we could stop by and give it to him." (Note that "stopping by" in this instance meant traveling thousands of miles, from Arrow's headquarters in Manitoba to the client's offices in Nova Scotia. That's another thing that makes Drew and Duane Ultimate Sales Professionals—they're willing to go the extra mile.)

Two weeks later, they were meeting with the CEO. He loved the shirt.

But Drew and Duane weren't there to sell shirts. They'd done their homework and came prepared to have a high-level conversation. They knew that hiring and retention of highly skilled workers was a huge challenge. The drilling company was well respected, but it was competing for talent against huge players, such as Exxon, BP, and Shell. Duane and Drew talked about strategic issues: elevating brand identity, building market visibility, fostering company pride, recognizing employee excellence. It was all music to the CEO's ears. Here were people who understood what he had to deal with!

One of the tactics that Drew and Duane recommended was a recognition program, providing employees with high-quality clothing and safety products. They explained how the program could build loyalty and goodwill with employees and potential recruits, while at the same time giving them greater visibility and exposure in the community and throughout the industry.

That meeting led to a million-dollar opportunity six months later.

These examples show that when USPs go after the right people—the buck stoppers—the results can be astounding. Less red tape. Faster decisions. Less focus on price and more emphasis on value. And in the end, bigger orders. But if you're going to talk to those people, you have to be prepared to speak their language. You can't be a product peddler. You have to understand their business from top to bottom and propose solutions that deliver extraordinary value.

14

EMBRACE THE MOMENT
OF TRUTH

I'm riding along with a salesperson as he calls on a customer. My job is simply to observe and, later, offer feedback. About six weeks ago, the rep submitted a proposal to the customer. Since then, they've had several follow-up meetings and phone calls.

At the meeting, I note that they seem to have good rapport. They chat about sports for a bit. Ask about each other's families. Catch up on industry gossip. I'm surreptitiously looking at my watch. Twenty minutes have already gone by.

Finally the rep sidles up to the business at hand. "So I sent over some revisions to the proposal, based on our last discussion. Did you get a chance to look them over?"

"I did," says the buyer.

"And what did you think?"

"We certainly seem to be moving in the right direction."

"Great. And did you have any questions?"

"Well, tell me about the warranty terms. What happens if something goes wrong, say, two days after the warranty expires?"

At which point the rep launches into a long-winded discussion of the post-warranty service options, the possibility of arranging an extended warranty, which would of course be an additional cost, the value that the rep's company places on long-term relationships and its willingness to work with customers to find a fair resolution of any disputes, and on and on.

Inside my head, I'm screaming, "Just ask for the order!" But I'm observing. I'm not supposed to say anything.

Before you know it, the buyer is saying, "So why don't you summarize all that in an email and I'll just run it by my boss to make sure he's OK with it."

Back in the car, I debriefed the rep. "How do you think that went?" I asked.

"I was disappointed that he's still dragging his heels. On the other hand, we're really, really close."

"Why do you say he's dragging his heels?"

"Well, he came up with that bogus question about the warranty."

"Yes, because you invited him to. Instead of asking if he had any questions, what if you'd just said, 'So how about it? Can we get started?' What would he have said?"

The rep thought about that for a while. "I don't know. Maybe no."

"That's true. He might have said no. In which case you'd be exactly where you are right now. Or he might have said yes. And you'd have a sale."

I read a shocking statistic the other day. It came from a massive study of more than one million sales calls, and it found that salespeople "ask for the order"—that is, ask the buyer to take the next step—only 13 percent of the time.

Think about that. As salespeople, we all get trained on call objectives. Before we communicate with a buyer, we're supposed to know exactly what action we want the buyer to take as a result. In transactional sales, it might be a decision to buy. In complex B2B selling, it more often means closing for the next step, which could be a follow-up meeting, an introduction to the boss, committing to a pilot or demo.

Yet in almost nine out of ten cases, salespeople *never ask their buyer to do the thing they want them to do.*

Why not? Salespeople will offer all sorts of reasons. They don't want to seem pushy. They didn't see a buying signal. The buyer raised an objection. And on and on.

I'm not buying it. I think the real reason is because they don't want to face the moment of truth. If they don't ask, the buyer can't say no. And the salesperson would rather live with a possible yes than a definite no.

NEVER FEAR THE TRUTH

•

USPs, on the other hand, *embrace* the moment of truth. Not just when it comes to closing, but in every part of their multifaceted relationships. Truth is liberating. It's empowering. And it's a powerful competitive advantage.

When you embrace the moment of truth—with customers, with colleagues, with bosses, with people in your personal life—you earn respect and multiply your effectiveness. Imagine if the rep I'd been coaching had just gone for it—if, instead of inviting the customer to take yet another ride on the sales merry-go-round, he'd said something like this: "I think this is a fair deal. It's going to get you what you need. So let's see if we can get it nailed down."

Or if the buyer had started worrying about the warranty, what if the salesperson had simply told the truth? "Look, if there are extenuating circumstances, we'll work with you. But if you're asking if we'll honor a warranty claim after the expiration date, no, that's not something I can promise." No hemming or hawing. Embrace the moment of truth, and buyers will see you as someone they can count on to always be straight with them.

A TRUTH-BASED CLOSING PROCESS

•

"Always Be Closing": I find that concept to be obnoxious. It reminds me of a three-year-old who thinks if he asks for a new toy enough times, Mom and Dad will eventually say yes. When a salesperson uses the ABC approach with me, it makes me *less* inclined to buy. Every question or statement coming out of the salesperson's mouth is designed to manipulate, corner, and overpower me. Sorry, not interested.

That's not what I'm talking about here. Asking for the order, or asking for the next step, isn't about imposing your will on the customer. It's about gathering information. If you've done your homework, identified the need, and presented a high-value proposition to the buyer, you've done all you can on your side. Now you need to know what's going on in the buyer's mind. And the only way to find out is to ask. You don't ask to pressure the buyer. You ask to understand the buyer.

That's why, in the moment of truth, a no is almost as good as a yes. If buyers say no, they'll almost always tell you why. Because you've asked for a decision, they have to be honest with you. If they say no, there has to be a reason. And that reason is the most valuable information you can ever get from buyers. It either tells you what you still need to do—"It looks great except for x, y, and z"—or it tells you to stop wasting your time—"It looks great but my boss hates your company and will never say yes."

There's a school of thought that says if you handle the sales process correctly, you don't need to close. Ask the right questions, get customers properly motivated, and they'll sell themselves.

Sometimes that happens. But not often. Customers as well as salespeople flinch at the moment of truth. They have as much on the line as you. Once they make a decision, they own it for better or worse. So unconsciously, they avoid it. That's why *you* need to ask.

If you don't, you may not get a second chance.

In today's fast-paced sales environment, opportunities can evaporate in an instant. Decision makers reconsider. Companies change direction. People change jobs. Customers who were ready to buy today could wake up tomorrow and conclude that this is a problem that can wait, while they turn their attention to the crisis du jour. If we are too skittish or anxious—if we let the moment of truth slip by and agree to follow up at a later date—chances are good that we've lost the sale.

What's more, when *we* aren't willing to face the truth, what does that say to buyers? Salespeople who lack the confidence to close come across as desperate. And customers don't want to entrust their needs and give their money to someone who's desperate or anxious.

If you're not confident of your recommendation, how can the buyer be? Next thing you know, they're hiding behind email and voice mail. If you ever find yourself wondering why a promising prospect suddenly went dark, consider whether it's because *you* planted the seeds of doubt.

BUYERS WANT AND NEED TO BE CLOSED

·

When salespeople fail to close, you have to wonder what buyers are thinking. "Is this salesperson ever going to get to the point? How long do we have to do this dance?" They have better things to do with their time. It's not their job to help you sell them. If you can't bring yourself to ask for the order, why should they give it to you?

I don't believe in being pushy, if *pushy* means putting my need for a sale ahead of the customer's need for a solution. But I do believe that I am serving my customers well when *I* take responsibility for moving the process forward. If they've articulated a need, I'm comfortable guiding them toward a solution and even persuading them to do what's right for them, their organization, and their goals. I can do that as long as I'm advocating for their needs first, and not mine.

Some prospects need to be told what to do. Some are too cautious and indecisive. There are times when you as a salesperson have to step in to lead, guide, direct, and motivate them to act: "If you don't address this issue, the potential risk for you and your organization could be profound. Here's what you need to do and why you need to do it."

I had my car in for service not long ago. My mechanic told me that the brake pads and rotors were shot. I said I'd get the brakes done at the next oil change. He looked at me and said: "That's not very smart. They need to be changed now."

Basically he was telling me I was being stupid. So was I mad at him? Did I feel he was being too pushy? Of course not. He was looking out for my safety and the safety of my family.

PERSONAL MOMENTS OF TRUTH

•

We face moments of truth in other areas of our careers and personal lives as well. "Should I take that new job?" "Do I have what it takes to go after big-ticket accounts?" "Am I really cut out for parenthood?"

Embracing the truth requires that you approach these decisions with an honest and realistic understanding of yourself.

The conventional wisdom on this issue, especially when it comes to salespeople, is that the biggest risk is overestimating your abilities. After all, everyone knows that salespeople have huge egos.

I see a more complex picture. Salespeople often *over*estimate their current capabilities but *under*estimate their potential capabilities. That's a recipe for getting stuck.

I've found many salespeople to be surprisingly risk averse. "I'm really good at selling widgets, but who knows if I'd be any good at selling something else?" Or, "I'm a really good farmer. I like managing existing accounts. If I tried to be a hunter, I could fail. I'll stick to what I know."

Don't mistake familiarity with competence. Don't assume that the thing you happen to be doing right now is the thing you're best at. You probably got where you are through some combination of interest, ability, and opportunity. A widget manufacturer needed a salesperson, and there you were. You got hired as an account manager and turned out to be pretty good at it. We all sort of fall into things. And that's fine, as long as we're willing to climb out at some point. All you know is what you've done. You don't know anything about what you haven't done.

DON'T SELL YOURSELF SHORT

Given a choice, it's better to overestimate your potential. If you believe you can do something, you may fail. But if you don't try, you may never discover your greatest strengths.

I'm not advocating foolish risks. Remember, we're talking about truth. And the best approach, I think, is also the most honest one: Believe you *might* be able to do it. In other words, try, but have a contingency plan. If you take this shot and fail, what happens? Don't bet the farm, but don't sell yourself short.

I wish I could go back in time about twenty or thirty years and give myself that advice.

I'm too old for false modesty. I turned out to be really good at things I never would have thought I was capable of. My greatest successes have come from thinking, "I might be able to do this." And my greatest regrets are about waiting too long to try something because I didn't feel "qualified," or believed I hadn't earned it yet, or that there were people who could do it far better.

I recall a time early in my career when I was teamed up with a colleague whose credentials far outshone my own. He had management skills and marketing know-how. He'd managed a huge operation in ten countries. All I knew how to do was sell. And I'd spent most of my career selling to small companies and mom-and-pop shops. I was intimidated, not by my colleague, who always treated me with courtesy and respect, but by myself. I cast myself in the role of student. It would be a great opportunity for me to learn from a master.

I did learn a lot. What I learned was that I had as much to teach as I did to learn. My colleague had certain strengths; I had others. Because of the way I'd come up in sales, I was scrappy. His approach was more cerebral; mine was very pragmatic. And I more than held my own.

Later, when I established my own practice, I didn't forget this experience. When I was meeting with sales VPs at multibillion-dollar companies, or competing against consultants who were much better known, I reminded myself not to sell myself short. I deserved to be where I was, doing what I was doing.

15

GIVING AND GETTING

Salespeople know better than anyone that you've got to give in order to get. And they give a lot. They give their time, their expertise, their commitment, their willingness to do whatever it takes to help customers succeed.

It's not altruism, of course. We do all this because we expect something in return. And not just a commission check. We expect our customers to reward us with their loyalty, their honesty, and their willingness to invest their own time, attention, and energy into the relationship.

This give-and-take—what psychologist and researcher Robert Cialdini calls the "law of reciprocity"—is one of the most fundamental principles governing human relations. Our brains are deeply programmed to maintain a mental scorecard of giving

THE ULTIMATE SALES PRO

and receiving, and to keep the books balanced. Of course we don't want to be taken advantage of (that is, giving more than we get). But for most of us, the opposite is also true. We don't want to take advantage. We don't want to be in anyone's debt. If someone gives us a gift, we feel obligated to do something in return. If we ask a favor, we're anxious to do one in return.

We clearly see this dynamic at social or family events. If you're invited to a wedding, you bring a gift. If a colleague takes you out to lunch and pays for the meal, you say, "Next time, my treat." If we're in a carpool, we insist on taking our turn behind the wheel. We don't want to be seen as a mooch.

DIFFERENT RULES

•

In a sales situation, the law of reciprocity still applies. But it works a little differently, because these are business relationships, not personal ones. When a salesperson takes prospects to lunch, those customers may not see the need to pick up the tab next time. Not because they're unsocialized, but because they think the salesperson is getting value *just from the relationship itself.* Buyers may honestly feel that their presence alone is reward enough. The salesperson's job is to schmooze buyers, so by allowing themselves to be schmoozed, they're helping the salesperson do his job. (I told you it was complicated.) In the customer's mind, the books are balanced. Ditto when the salesperson provides above-and-beyond service. The customer thinks: "That's part of what we pay for. I appreciate all the hard work, but I haven't incurred a social debt that must be repaid."

And let's face it: Salespeople *aren't* doing these nice things just out of the goodness of their heart. They *want* buyers to feel obligated, because then maybe they'll buy something or reward salespeople with their loyalty.

Now, there's nothing wrong with any of this, as long as everyone understands the rules. Where it *does* become a problem is when salespeople and buyers have different expectations. For example, when a prospect allows him- or herself to be wined and dined but never ends up buying anything, some salespeople take it personally. When salespeople give up a weekend to help a buyer out of a jam, they expect the buyer to reward them by giving them more business. And when it doesn't happen, salespeople are often offended. Buyers, in turn, sense the resentment. Or they feel manipulated. Trust erodes. What should be a mutually beneficial relationship turns into a mutually suspicious relationship.

Ultimate Sales Professionals don't get offended. They don't take things personally. They recognize that this is a business relationship. They don't expect people to buy out of a sense of social obligation. They want buyers to buy because of value.

And because it *is* a business relationship, USPs are not in the habit of giving without getting. They're positive and polite, but they're explicit about their expectations.

Guess what: When you're up front about what you expect, buyers respect that. Because you've avoided the potential for misunderstandings. Relationships are stronger when everyone understands the rules.

FREE HAS NO VALUE

•

When I was starting out in my business, I thought free was a good way to get off on the right foot with prospects: "I'll give your team a free workshop so you can experience firsthand what we can do for you." "I'll fly out to meet you and your team at my own expense to give you a presentation." I'd contact a trade association and be told, "Well, we don't pay speakers or cover expenses. But if you want to build your network, we'll let you come in and we won't even charge you for the conference." My attitude was, "Why not?"

I was new in the business and needed the visibility. And what did I have to lose? Just some money and time—but hey, that was the cost of doing business.

Well, after a few of these experiences, I figured out that giving stuff away did not get me more business. In fact, I'm convinced that it *cost* me business, because it devalued the very thing I was trying to get people to pay for.

When you give without getting anything in return, you actively undermine your value. Remember, we all keep a mental balance sheet. And if we get something for free, one way to balance the books is by discounting the value of whatever it is we received.

You've experienced it yourself: A telemarketer calls you with a "free" offer: two nights in a luxury hotel if you'll listen to their time-share pitch. In the mail, you get a "free" discount card that saves you money on prescriptions. Or you get an email offering a free trial subscription to a magazine. Because they're free, you immediately start discounting them: "Oh, the rooms are free because the hotel is empty that time of year." "The prescription discounts probably don't apply to the medicines I use." "The magazines will sit there because I'm too busy to read them." So thanks, but no thanks.

DON'T CONSULT FOR FREE

•

Bordertown Retail Systems manufactures and sells metal racks for retail displays. One day the sales manager, Ian Symington, called me up and said he had a big prospect who'd agreed to let him come in and do a free lunch-and-learn, a session where a vendor goes into a company, educates the staff, and feeds them lunch. He wanted me to coach him on how to deliver an effective program.

Lots of vendors do lunch-and-learns. As part of a broader marketing strategy, they can be effective, especially if you have a new or unfamiliar product that people don't understand. But I always have to ask: Are people there because they feel the need to get educated on this product? Or are they there for the free lunch?

In most cases, you're discounting your own expertise. You're giving away free advice to too many people who are not qualified or interested in what you have to offer. And the costs are not insignificant. A dozen or two lunches. Travel expenses. And that's the least of it. The real expense is the opportunity cost. Ian spent a week preparing his forty-five minute presentation, meaning he had to postpone other sales calls. There was probably $20,000 worth of business he did not close that week because he was getting ready for the lunch-and-learn.

But the biggest cost was to his perceived value. When Ian got there, half the folks who were supposed to be there didn't show up, especially the key decision makers, who were all suddenly too busy to attend. Mostly he got low-level employees who had nothing better to do than listen to his spiel, and other hangers-on who had no business being there at all. As Ian tried to get through his slides, the audience was munching away, looking at their phones, chatting with one another.

Did he get positive feedback afterward? Sure. People said they got some great ideas about how to design retail displays for maximum effectiveness. But what message did Ian's efforts send to the real decision makers at the company? Did it position Ian as a heavy hitter, an expert on retail displays who could boost their bottom line? Or as a guy chasing their business, who happened to have some interesting ideas?

It really was a lunch-and-learn—for Ian. He learned that he should demand more in exchange for his hard-won knowledge and expertise.

When his client offered him the "opportunity" to do a lunch-and-learn, he might have said something like this:

"Thanks for the opportunity, but I have to be forthright: Our experience is that lunch-and-learns are often distracting and a little unruly.

"Here's what we can offer instead: We've recently worked with several clients to redesign their retail displays, resulting in a 25 percent acceleration in inventory turns. Help me set up a meeting with the right person in your organization, and I'm confident we can make that happen for you."

In other words, giving and getting: You're willing to give the buyer the value of your expertise if you can get a meeting with a real decision maker.

USPs are willing to say no to low-value situations and propose something better. They *will* invest their time, but only as long as the buyer reciprocates with equal value—for example, the time and attention of high-level decision makers.

OVER-THE-TOP SERVICE?

●

One of my clients is an electrical distributor. The sales manager, Tim, has very good relationships with his customers. It's common for him to get a call like this on any given morning:

"Tim, I don't have Part XYZ-2001 in stock. One of my customers is here at the counter and needs it. Can you run over and drop off a box for me?"

What's Tim supposed to do? Rework his schedule for the morning? Put off seeing two other customers he'd planned to call on so he can drop off that box?

If he does, the customer is sure to give Tim a big thanks. He'll feel a little sheepish. He'll say, "I hope I didn't put you out of your way."

An ordinary salesperson would jump on this opportunity to be a hero. "No problem," he'd say. "I was in the neighborhood anyway."

Later he'd tell himself: "Good for me. I made my customer happy. I reinforced the relationship. I gave him one more reason to do business with us."

But what the salesperson is really doing is reinforcing this behavior. No matter that the customer didn't plan correctly, let his inventories get low, or couldn't be bothered to reorder last month. The salesperson will bail him out.

A USP is willing to go the extra mile but expects more than a pat on the back. She might say something like this: "Sure, I'll run it right over. And since I'm coming over anyway, let's schedule a few minutes to go over x and y. I have some ideas to get you more exposure and more customers. And while we're at it, let's check your inventory to be sure you don't run out of anything else."

The USP's number-one objective is to sell. Servicing is not selling. So they turn service calls into sales calls. The customer is happy; you're helping him out of a bind. So ask for something. "Hey, while I'm here, can we stop in and chat with your boss for a minute? Can we talk about next year? Can I show you our new product?"

And when there's no opportunity to turn a service call into a sales opportunity, delegate instead. Tim, for example, is worth $3 million in sales revenue for the year. That works out to about $1,200 per hour. At those rates, Tim should not be driving a delivery truck. Especially when he can get one of the people in the warehouse to do it instead.

Every hour spent on non-selling activities is costing him and his company money in terms of opportunity costs. If Tim's not careful, he'll be scurrying around like a squirrel. He's got to be diligent, focused, and protective of his time, and not let customers or management take it from him.

Let me be clear: USPs don't shirk responsibility. They make sure their customers get great service. They organize company resources to get problems resolved and follow up to make sure it stays fixed. But they can't be superheroes. Delegating responsibilities to other team members is scary. You might lose control. Somebody may screw it up. And frankly, it's hard to watch someone else be the hero to *your* customer while you're out getting hammered, rejected, and pummeled as you try to bring in more business. But that's your job. It's the most important one. And it's the one that *can't* be delegated.

RFPS: ASKING WITHOUT GIVING

I don't know who invented the request-for-proposal (RFP), but it's one of the biggest rackets in business today. A company sends out a vague document, often with no actual commitment to buy anything, and sits back while vendors fall all over themselves responding.

USPs don't take RFPs seriously. They see them for what they are: BS, smoke screens, a façade that buyers hide behind.

That doesn't mean that USPs ignore the RFP. But they feel no obligation to follow rules that they never agreed to. They only use it as a springboard for conversation. If an RFP arrives on their doorstep from a company that they'd like to do business with, they don't start filling out the forms. They pick up the phone, call the person listed on the RFP, and say, "Hey, thanks for thinking of us. I have a few questions about that RFP you sent over."

Their questions are designed to find out what's really going on. Why did the company put together the RFP? What triggered it? With some direct questions, you can usually flush out the truth. Perhaps something is going on with the existing vendor relationship. Or maybe there's a new face in Purchasing who wants to justify his or her job by shaking things up. Ideally, there are real business reasons driving the effort: some underlying threat in the market or some new opportunity. If the contact can't or won't give you a straight answer, figure out how to reach out to a key decision maker and have a real conversation: "So about this RFP, what are you trying to do? Tell me more about . . . . Why is this an issue all of a sudden? How is this problem affecting you, your company, your colleagues?"

You get the idea. USPs use the RFP to build a relationship, weave things together, find out something other vendors don't know. So when you make a recommendation, the buyer is thinking: "Wow! You know us better than we know ourselves. You've identified problems that we never even considered. You made us think." At that point, the RFP is almost completely irrelevant.

However, some folks don't want you looking under their covers, whether it's because of shame over how they run their business, lack of desire to really resolve the issue, a hidden agenda, office politics, a desire for free consulting, or because they don't want to tell you that they just need three quotes before they give the business to the vendor they really want to use.

You don't have time for that. If someone wants to do business with you, they have to give you the truth.

Does that seem too aggressive? Will it put off the prospect? Well, what do you have to lose, really? You're not likely to win the business anyway if you don't have good information. You might get lucky. But if you want to roll the dice, go to a casino. The odds are better.

THE COURAGE TO SAY NO

•

The other day, someone called and asked me to come in and meet with his executives about putting together a sales training program. It seemed like a great opportunity: A prestigious company. Close to home. Talking to decision makers.

Then he asked, "So what do you charge?"

I gave him an honest answer: "I don't know what I'd charge, because I have no idea what you need or want. But since you raised the question, let me ask: What kind of budget are you working with?"

Long pause. "I don't know. My boss hasn't set a budget."

This is a game I no longer play.

"Look," I said. "If you don't have a budget, I'm not comfortable coming in for a day to spend time with you and your people trying to diagnose your problems. If it turned out the budget is too low, then there's a good chance I wouldn't be a good fit. It wouldn't be fair to waste your execs' time. Before we set up a meeting, why don't you go back to your boss and get some ballpark numbers?"

I was being diplomatic, but I was basically telling him, "You've got to give me information if I'm going to give you a day of my time."

Guess what? He did. And he had no hard feelings. I'd simply explained the rules by which I operate. The numbers were workable, and we were off to a great start.

So how about you? Have you ever evaluated a prospect's current operations or system, spent hours to diagnose the problem and develop a recommendation, only to have them take your proposal and shop it around to other suppliers to get a cheaper price? Or leave you hanging without ever making a yes or no decision?

If so, repeat after me: "I will never give away my knowledge and expertise without getting something of equal value in return."

USPs learn to charge for their services. I'm not necessarily talking about sending them a bill for your time. But if you're going to give something, ask for what you want or need in return—a meeting with a decision maker, a promise not to shop your solution around, a commitment to move forward if your proposal makes sense. Of course, a prospect could always renege. But when you (1) make your expectations clear and (2) get agreement, you activate the law of reciprocity. Most prospects will feel obligated to balance the books.

16

CHANGE LIVES

When I was five years old, my dad lost his job. For the next six months, he drove a taxi in New York City to support my mom and his kids. Then he bought a hearing aid franchise in Wilmington, Delaware. Six months later, the parent company went bankrupt. He was still stuck with the downtown storefront and had to take on other product lines to stay afloat.

The following year, 1968, riots were ripping through downtown Wilmington. The city was falling apart. We had National Guard troops patrolling the streets. The public schools were unsafe. My parents pulled me out and sent me to Catholic school. They thought it would be a refuge for me.

It wasn't. The old-school nuns who ran the school ruled through fear. They had a picture of an eye on the front wall of the classroom. It meant that God was watching you. Step out of line, and God would punish you. If God didn't, the nuns would.

I didn't fit in. I was bullied, lonely, and depressed. Because I lived in a slightly nicer neighborhood than most of the other students, they thought my family was rich (we weren't). I had no friends. Every day walking to school, I had to take different routes to avoid being followed or jumped.

At home, whenever I tried to express my unhappiness, I'd hear about how much harder it had been for my parents when they grew up. I wanted my mom to listen, but she always turned the tables to talk about her struggles, her pains, her unhappiness, her depression. She'd lost her sister when she was young. And then her mom a few years later. Was raised in a boarding school. Immigrated to America from England all by herself. I couldn't compete with her suffering, so I clammed up. My dad was a good man but quiet and aloof. He had his own challenges. He dealt with life by tuning things out.

I hated my life. I ended up confiding in a priest in high school, who had the wisdom to suggest that I needed professional help. But the school had no counselors to talk to. It was up to me to find the help I needed.

And so I took it upon myself to make a few calls. I found a therapist nearby and called. When I met Dr. Joyce Weber, she explained that I was supposed to get my parents' consent since I was under eighteen. I explained that they'd freak out if they knew I was seeing a therapist. Dr. Weber listened, said she understood, and bent the rules to take me as an outpatient.

I met with her for two years, and she probably saved my life.

Her only tools were her ability to listen, empathize, and ask questions. She couldn't "cure" me with drugs or surgery. She couldn't even tell me what to do. But her artful questions helped me fix myself. They helped reveal how my own thinking was holding me back; how to channel my raw, ugly emotions into positive energy; how to confront my demons and fears; and how to articulate my dreams and hopes for a better future. Sometimes the questions were painful. Sometimes I'd spend an entire session trying not to answer them. But answer them I did. And that's what made me better.

PROFOUND QUESTIONS

•

I tell you this story because the power of questioning and listening changed my life. It's why I live, teach, and breathe the power of questioning and listening. It's just as important in the business world as in our personal lives. Customers want what everyone wants: to be heard and understood. They want to gripe, vent, and expose their vulnerabilities, fears, and anxieties.

A question seems like such a simple thing. But the right question at the right time can be profound. Are you happy with the way things are? Are you willing to make a change? What's keeping you from doing so? What are you proud of? What's important to you? What are you afraid of?

Do questions like these strike you as out of place in a sales conversation? Do they seem too personal? I don't think so. The best salespeople I know are willing to dig deep with their customers. They get buyers talking about things that truly matter.

After all, aren't buyers really looking for an opportunity to make things better in some way for themselves or someone else? They're not writing you a check so you can make your quota, or because they have so much money that they don't know what to do with it. Every sale represents a choice on the part of the buyer. When they buy from you, they're giving up something else they could have bought with their hard-earned money. They chose you because they're hoping you can make their life better.

Don't underestimate your power to change lives through what you sell.

There's a big company near me—SPS Technologies. It makes and sells the most boring products you could imagine: Bolts. Screws. Rivets. Little pieces of steel that hold pieces of metal together. Manufacturing companies buy them by the truckload. Hardly the sort of thing that would be life changing, right?

Well, unless you're ten thousand feet in the air.

Genuine fasteners go through a rigorous quality-control system to ensure that they won't fail. It's easy enough to knock off a cheap copy that looks identical to the real thing but is made from inferior materials.

Back in the 1980s and 1990s, counterfeiting was rampant in the industry. The Federal Aviation Administration documented that 166 aviation accidents and incidents had been caused by counterfeit parts. In 1989, a turboprop plane crashed into the North Sea, killing fifty-five people, because of counterfeit bolts used in the tail section. In 1990, a U.S. parts distributor was convicted of selling counterfeit fasteners to major airlines, airplane manufacturers, and even the Israeli government.

Imagine you were the technician who unknowingly installed those fake fasteners on the turboprop that crashed. It wasn't your fault, but your actions led to dozens of people dying. Imagine you were a passenger on that plane, or a loved one waiting at the terminal.

SPS was one of the first in the industry to implement a rigorous registration system. Every rivet it sells comes with a pedigree, which follows it throughout the supply chain, all the way from manufacturing to installation. Manufacturers and repair crews can be confident that the fasteners they're using are the genuine article. These products save lives.

Now, wouldn't that be something worth selling?

Here's another example:

When I was selling Yellow Pages ads, I had the opportunity to get to know the small-business owners I served. I asked questions and listened to their stories. People had risked their life savings to open a plumbing service or pizza shop or dry-cleaning business. It was how they put food on the table, paid the mortgage, put their kids through college. Many told me how their dads and moms had founded the business and struggled to make it a success, and how they now felt a deep sense of responsibility to keep it going.

What was my goal when selling Yellow Pages ads? To sell every customer the program that would put the most money in my pocket? Not so. My goal was to sell them the program that would do the best job of keeping their businesses open and healthy. Now, it was certainly in my interest to keep their businesses healthy so they could come back and buy more ads year after year. It was also useful for me to have success stories I could share with other prospects. But there was more to it than that.

What really gave me a boost was when customers actually thanked me and talked about how I'd helped keep their business healthy and helped them and their families achieve their dreams. I truly was changing lives.

And these days, I get the same feeling when I help turn losses into profit for a company whose sales were struggling or coach a struggling salesperson who was ready to throw in the towel by offering ideas to reenergize and perhaps salvage his or her career. Make no mistake: I'm running a business, and I like getting paid for what I do. But making a difference in people's lives? Man, it doesn't get any better than that.

17

IT'S NOT WHO YOU KNOW—
IT'S WHO KNOWS YOU

In 2006, the bottom fell out of my business.

I'd been a successful sales trainer for nineteen years and a successful salesperson for many years before that. I'd launched my own training company in 2003, and now I had a long list of high-profile clients I'd worked with. I'd just published my first book. I had a downtown office, a nice car, a nice house, a wonderful family, and great client relationships. I was my own boss. I'd worked hard to get to this place in my life, and I was content.

Then one day, my contact at our largest client told me the company was about to be sold.

"Nothing to worry about," he reassured me. "The new owners bought us because we're successful. They'll leave us alone."

Of course, they didn't. In three months, the entire senior management staff was gone, including all the people I'd been working with.

As a sales pro, I knew what I had to do: I had to quickly engage with the new management team, build new relationships, and show them how much value I could continue to add to the company.

That was the plan, anyway. But I never stood a chance.

Those great relationships I'd cultivated with the previous management team now worked against me. I was damaged goods. I couldn't get anyone to take my call, much less build a relationship. All I got was a letter canceling my contract.

I'd made the mistake that plagues so many small businesses: I put too many of my eggs in one basket. Of course I knew the risks and had planned to diversify my client base. But when you have a customer who loves you, needs your help, and can pay for it, it's hard to say no.

I tapped into my network. I called former clients. Made tons of cold calls. But by then the economy had started to sour. Companies were looking for ways to cut costs, not take on new ones.

Meanwhile, I was having nightmares about my own balance sheet. My wife had just quit her career to be a stay-at-home mom and raise our two daughters. I had a mortgage, office rent, two car payments. And I was bleeding money.

I closed my office. I sold one car and thought I might have to sell the other one. I was eating through my savings at an alarming rate. With no prospective clients on the horizon, I was close to shutting down my business altogether. But as I looked at the rising unemployment rate, I wondered if I'd even be able to find a job. Any job.

Then one day my phone rang.

The call was from an acquaintance I'd met several years earlier at a conference. Like me, he was a trainer, but in a different field. We'd kept in touch for a while, trading ideas and contacts. But we were by no means close friends, and I hadn't heard from him for a long time.

Now he was telling me that he knew of a large pharmaceutical company that was looking for sales training. He'd thought of me, knowing that I'd worked in medical sales. "I can get you a meeting and put in a good word for you," he said. "Are you interested?"

Long story short, I got the contract and saved my business.

HOW TO MAKE YOUR OWN LUCK

Why do I tell this story? Because of what I learned: Sales skills alone are not always enough to succeed in sales. I knew how to prospect, how to close, how to create good client relationships and build value. But when my back was against the wall, I needed something more.

The truth is, I needed a lucky break, and I got one just in time. But luck doesn't come out of the blue. Years earlier, I'd made a little extra effort to connect with this person. I didn't give it much thought at the time. We had mutual interests. I thought I might be helpful to him, and that I might learn something in return. I certainly had no reason to think this connection would one day save my business. But it did.

Every successful person I know can tell a similar story. At a critical point in their career, they caught a break. Somebody helped them out, introduced them to the right person, showed them how to solve a problem or simply believed in them. You can call it luck, but in nearly every case, that "luck" was rooted in a relationship.

IT'S NOT JUST WHAT YOU KNOW . . .

•

In the end, success in sales or anything else requires more than being good at your job. In fact, as I learned, there really is no such thing as a casual encounter. Everyone you come across is an opportunity for you to enrich your life—and, not coincidentally, build your sales.

According to the old adage, "It's whom you know." That's not entirely true, of course. Your network of contacts isn't much good if you can't deliver the goods. But every salesperson knows that, in the end, sales is about people and relationships.

Good salespeople work hard to cultivate relationships with buyers and prospects. Ultimate Sales Pros go further. They cultivate relationships with as many people as they can. They see *every* encounter as an opportunity to build their personal and professional network.

Some salespeople resist that notion. They don't want to be that obnoxious salesperson who's handing out business cards at a wedding or strong-arming friends and acquaintances. But that's not networking. Nobody wants to be an unpaid member of your prospecting team. Nobody wants to feel like a mark.

What they *will* respond to is someone who's genuinely interested in them as a person, someone who sees value in the relationship itself. For me, that's a liberating concept. I don't need to worry about what I'm getting out of the relationship. The connection itself is what's important.

When you're networking, that's the most valuable thing you can offer someone: your sincere curiosity.

What's more, I find that I *always* learn something new when I connect with new people and ask them about themselves. Most people are dying for someone to be interested in them: What they think, what they do for a living, how they got where they are today. Their spouses, kids, colleagues, and/or friends have heard all their stories. At cocktail parties, nobody seems to be too interested in hearing about the challenges they face as the assistant controller for an industrial distribution company.

But I usually find those details fascinating, and I'm not just asking out of politeness. Perhaps because I'm in a problem-solving business, I'm deeply interested in the challenges ordinary people face, how they respond to them, and, perhaps most important, how they *feel* about them. I'm curious about what assistant controllers at industrial distribution companies do, because it's something I know very little about. And, who knows, perhaps one day I'll be talking to the assistant controller for one of my clients or prospects and be able to use what I've learned.

Here's my challenge to you: In the next week, strike up a conversation with someone you've just met, or someone you don't know well. It could be anyone. Someone at work in another department. A customer or prospect. The librarian at your public library. The person who's renovating your kitchen. Start with simple stuff—the weather, last weekend's football game, where he or she lives. Then go a little deeper. Ask a question that opens you up to this person's world, one that reveals something about his or her goals, values, or struggles. How did this person get into this line of work? What part of work is most enjoyable? What's your librarian's favorite book? What's the most unusual job your contractor ever worked on? Would he or she rather swing a hammer or build a business? Do this with no agenda other than simple curiosity. Don't try to fix problems or offer advice. Simply listen.

It's amazing how transformational that curiosity can feel to the other person. I guarantee that he or she will remember the conversation and you. Now imagine having those conversations with people in your professional world. Again, no selling, no agenda, just curiosity and a willingness to listen. You learn something, and you make an impression.

The ability to listen is the most important skill you have as a salesperson. Ordinary salespeople listen for sales opportunities. Ultimate Sales Pros listen for understanding.

18

TAKE CARE OF YOUR INTERNAL CUSTOMERS

Some of your most important customers are the ones within your organization.

Many salespeople don't give these relationships their due. They believe that, if they're not talking to buyers, they're not making money.

For the most part, selling requires independence and resilience. Sometimes there's an overreliance on self-sufficiency: "I don't need help, I can do it all myself"; "I'm the one who makes things happen."

But consider what your job really is as a salesperson. You serve as the link between two organizations: your customer's and your own. Throughout this book, I've talked about the idea that great salespeople create value. The way they do it is by connecting customer needs with their company's offerings.

To make that Value Equation work (see Chapter Eleven to refresh your memory), you need to cultivate relationships on both sides of the table. I can't count how many times I've heard salespeople complain that they'd lined up a great sale, only to have the idiots back at their home office screw it up. Somebody balked at the price concession they wanted to offer or refused to move heaven and earth to meet the customer's impossible delivery date, or took too long to approve the deal, or dropped the ball on a service issue and put a major account in jeopardy.

Salespeople tend to view such things as failures of the company, and they take it personally. "With all these knuckleheads I have to deal with, it's a wonder I can sell anything at all," they tell themselves.

Here's the reality: In nearly every case, these are failures of the salesperson. After all, who's supposed to be the expert at getting buy-in and cooperation? Whose job is it to keep sales moving? Who has the skills to motivate people, overcome objections, demonstrate value, and inspire people to take action?

Salespeople.

So if they can't get their own organization to buy in, they've only done half their job.

Ultimate Sales Pros work hard to cultivate internal relationships—with their bosses, their colleagues in sales, the people who will create and deliver what they sell, the person who answers the phone, all the way up to the person who signs the checks.

They win more sales because everyone in their organization has their back.

YOUR MOST IMPORTANT CUSTOMER

•

Some salespeople don't like their bosses, don't respect them, or are fearful of them. Many are reluctant to bring their bosses out into the field because the boss might embarrass or antagonize the customer or say something that could screw up the sale. Some salespeople don't believe they need a boss. But who's going to keep them grounded, make sure sales reports get done, orders get processed, margins are maintained, and orders stay flowing?

Treat your boss as if he or she is your most important customer. As Zig Ziglar used to say, "You can have everything in life that you want if you just help other people get what they want." So start by understanding what your boss really wants and needs.

More sales, obviously. But that's a given, like a prospect who tells you, "We need to lower costs." You have to dig deeper than that. What is he or she being judged on? Do you know the key performance indicators? What keeps your boss awake at night?

For example, maybe your boss needs to add two new salespeople this year to meet the sales target. That's a high-risk issue. There's pressure from the top to fill those slots, but a bad hire is disastrous.

Finding good candidates is not, strictly speaking, your problem. But if it were your customer, wouldn't you want to lend a hand if you could? If you can help your boss solve a problem, it's not sucking up. It's customer management.

BE A SERVANT LEADER

•

Leadership isn't a matter of who reports to whom. It's a matter of whom people are willing to follow. For you, that means all the people who could potentially affect your sale. You never know when you might need the receptionist to track you down because your customer is on the line with an emergency. You never know when someone in engineering has a brother-in-law who happens to work at the company you've been trying to get into for the past year. You never know when you're going to get called into the CEO's office to explain why a major account just gave notice. So you'd better understand what matters to people and think about how you can help them get it.

Great leaders embrace the idea of "servant leadership." Their job is to serve the people in their organization—to help those people get what they want and need. That's what makes people follow a leader and be willing to go the extra mile for them.

What most people want and need isn't that hard to give. They want acknowledgment, respect, and understanding. They want you to know their name and what they do. They want to be told when they do a good job and thanked when they go above and beyond, with a note to their boss, if possible. They also want to be in the loop, to know why the customer needs what you're asking for. They want you to listen when they're trying to explain something to you. They want you to know how hard they work. Sometimes they just want a sympathetic ear. And it doesn't hurt to know the names of their kids, or whether they have any.

STAND UP FOR YOURSELF

•

Sometimes, of course, you have to deal with a boss, peers, or leadership that doesn't act with integrity or honesty. Peers may undermine you because they're competing for the same business. Management doesn't keep its word; someone decides the comp structure is too generous or the quotas are too low. Bosses can be inaccessible, overbearing, incompetent, or manipulative. Then what do you do?

You already know what to do. You have customers who lie to you, cut their budgets, break their promises, sell you out. It doesn't mean you refuse to do business with them. You manage them. If you're confident of the unique value you offer, and confident that they understand that value (even if they won't admit it), you can insist on being treated fairly. You remain respectful, but ask hard questions, and keep asking to get the clarity you deserve. You can say no to unreasonable demands. Whether customers or bosses, most bullies back down if you refuse to play their game. They look for easier targets.

And if it continues, the question you need to ask yourself is, "Am I getting enough value out of this relationship to justify the cost?" If not, start looking for an exit strategy. Some people just aren't worth doing business with.

19

TOOT YOUR HORN

When It comes to any discussion of branding and self-promotion, salespeople need to proceed cautiously. I'm inundated with advice that salespeople need to tweet more, post more, blog more, write more, speak more, and on and on. If you listened to all the advice coming from social media platforms and consultants, you wouldn't have time to sell. And in the end, selling is what's going to make or break your reputation.

Salespeople *do* have to promote themselves. They need to be visible to their markets and potential buyers. But you can't compete with the big boys. Some companies have rooms full of people who tweet, blog, and post all day long. They spend huge amounts of money to raise their visibility on search engines and get themselves in front of people looking to buy. You don't have enough time or money to elbow your way to the top of that heap.

Fortunately, you don't have to.

They're looking for the broadest possible reach. You just need to get yourself known to the people who matter to your business. They're like the big box retailer. You're like the local hardware store. They're marketing to the world. You're marketing to the neighborhood.

These days, of course, the "neighborhood" is no longer defined by geography. For the Ultimate Sales Pro, it's your professional network, including customers (present and past), potential customers, people in your industry (especially influencers), and all the people they know.

In Chapter Six, I wrote about the power of profiling, and how much more effective your prospecting becomes when you narrow your focus and target high-potential prospects. The same rule applies to marketing and self-promotion. When you filter your audience down to the people who really matter, the list gets short quickly. It might be three hundred, five hundred, or one thousand people at its core, and perhaps several thousand more in a secondary role.

For the big marketers, that's an audience too small to target. But for an individual practitioner, those are manageable numbers. At that scale, you can afford to do what the big boys can't: apply a personal touch. Instead of blasting emails to a purchased list and hoping someone responds, for example, you can build your own list of actual high-value contacts and cultivate them one-on-one.

Social media and other tools still play a role in this effort, but you can use them in a much more purposeful and efficient way. For example, if you find an article or blog post online that you think would be valuable for your network, you can do more than retweet it to the world at large and hope somebody stumbles across it. You can retweet it and then send personalized emails to your contacts: "Hey, I ran across this and it reminded me of the conversation we had last week. I wanted you to see it."

Here are some additional high-return ways you can build your personal brand:

POLISH YOUR ONLINE PERSONA

It's an eye-opener to Google your name and see what comes up. It's painful when you can't find yourself (or, worse, find something negative). So buff up your online presence. Write a few articles. Post a YouTube video of you doing a demonstration or interviewing a customer. Your goal isn't to pop up every time someone is looking to buy what you sell; it's about controlling your public persona and what people see when they're checking you out online.

A little bit of effort can go a long way. *Recency* and *reputation* are the most important factors in what shows up at the top of the search results—for example, if you've recently been featured in a story from a trade magazine or bylined an article on your company blog. Other outlets to consider: white papers, ebooks, webinars, especially in your industry. They create buzz and the opportunity for potential customers to find you.

SOCIAL MEDIA: BEWARE THE BLACK HOLE

•

Be disciplined and judicious with social media. Focus on the opportunities that deliver the best bang for the buck. Retweeting or commenting on marginal content may not get you much and may actually make you seem opportunistic or unfocused. A well-crafted comment on a respected thought leader's post, by contrast, may have a wider reach and enhance your reputation.

When it comes to the mechanics of social media and promotion, it's often worth hiring people who can do it better than you, thus freeing up time for you to focus on selling. Again, I'm not talking about big-ticket items here, just basic blocking and tackling. Most of us have a presence on LinkedIn. It's our business card, résumé, credentials. Consider hiring someone who can make it look professional and compelling. The price is usually reasonable.

LEVERAGE YOUR MARKETING DEPARTMENT

•

Despite all the reported bad blood between marketing and sales, here's a secret about your marketing department: They love you. And if you ask the right way, they'll bend over backward to promote your personal brand right alongside your company's brand.

The reason: You add the human touch. People are more persuasive than companies. And what better face to put on their marketing efforts than someone who is already out there interacting with customers and driving revenue for the company?

Depending on the resources available, here are some ways your marketing department may be able to help you:

- Case histories and testimonials featuring your customers (with their permission, of course)
- Announcements of major sales (again, with the customers' permission)
- Speaking opportunities, for example, at industry events
- Ghostwriting blogs, posts, articles, and editorials in your name
- Enhancing your LinkedIn profile
- Creating and managing social media content, comments for you
- Personalized email campaigns to your customers and prospects
- Outreach to trade show attendees
- Setting up plant tours or other events

MAXIMIZE TRADE SHOWS

A lot of salespeople hate trade shows. You're on your feet in the booth all day, chatting with tire-kickers, when you could be out selling. If you draw the short straw and have to work the booth all day, you have my sympathy.

But there are better ways to take advantage of trade shows. It really is an opportunity to build your visibility in the "neighborhood" and create face-to-face encounters. The key is to get out of the booth. Are there influencers or prospects you've been trying to reach? Reach out to them a few weeks before the show, find out if they're attending, and make a plan to meet. Even the busiest attendees will often be willing to sit down in a quiet corner for a few minutes to rest their feet and have a cup of coffee.

You can take advantage of these opportunities even if your company isn't exhibiting. In fact, that's better in some ways, because you don't have to worry about booth duty. If the conference is expensive, you may be able to get a ticket to just the exhibition floor for a nominal cost. That will serve your networking purposes almost as well.

STALK YOUR CUSTOMERS

•

I don't mean follow them home. I'm talking about learning where they hang out, professionally speaking. Where would they—and people with similar needs and interests—be likely to bump into you? What LinkedIn groups do they belong to? What industry associations are they involved with, and which ones do they find most valuable? Who do they follow on Twitter?

And where would you get such information? Well, from customers themselves, of course! The next time you meet with a buyer, ask the question: "I'd like to get more involved in the industry. What associations would you recommend? Which ones do you belong to? What events do you attend? Which local chapters are most active? What LinkedIn groups do you belong to?"

REDISCOVER THE LOST ART
OF NETWORKING

•

While we're on the subject, I believe that networking (including membership in associations) is one of the most underutilized marketing opportunities for building your personal brand. Americans used to be joiners, but they're far less so today. Everybody seems to be too busy, and frankly there are many more enjoyable ways to spend your time.

But top professionals never miss an opportunity to network. They're active in their industries. They sit on boards of charities. They go to fund-raising dinners. One reason, apart from altruism, is because they know that other master networkers will be doing the same thing.

Try to be more than just a passive member. Volunteer for one of their many committees. As you get comfortable, consider taking on a more visible leadership role; for example, become a facilitator or presenter for a workshop session. Associations in particular are challenged to retain and grow their membership base and will be happy to have you involved. Many lack resources and manpower and depend on volunteers. What you get in return is the opportunity to network with members of the board and executive committee, who typically are movers and shakers.

BE AN ORGANIZER

•

There are always things that need to be organized, and nobody wants the job. If you take on the responsibility of organizing, say, an event for a local association chapter, imagine how much visibility that could create in your market. If you volunteer to host a meeting at your office, consider how much value you'd get out of having people see your operations and what you do.

You can do the same thing on an informal basis as well. You might organize an industry softball league. A networking event. A dinner where your top customers can rub elbows with one another.

LISTEN MORE, TALK LESS

•

I believe in elevator speeches. But I'd never deliver one in an actual elevator. First of all, that would be creepy; nobody talks to strangers in an elevator. Second of all, random people just aren't that interested in what I do for a living. If I'm in a situation where people *are* likely to be interested—at a networking event, for example, or a trade show, or especially on a prospecting call—I'll offer a fifteen- to twenty-second summary of what I do and how I create value.

But even in those situations, I keep it short and sweet, just enough to help orient the other people to who I am and what I do. I'm far more interested in hearing the other people's elevator speech. It's amazing: What makes *you* memorable to other people is when you shut up and listen to *their* story.

"That Paul Cherry—he's a fascinating guy," they tell their friends.

"What's so fascinating about him?" their friends ask.

"Well, I can't say exactly. But we had a great conversation!"

Don't underestimate the branding power of these sorts of encounters. As I've said, your advantage over the big marketers is the personal touch. What's going to have a bigger impact on people: a clever email sent to me and five million others—or a one-on-one conversation with someone who gets me?

20

BUILD A REFERRAL BUSINESS

One of my clients, Brookaire Company, sells HVAC parts and supplies. It's not a sexy business, so they differentiate on quality, service, and reliability.

One day not long ago, the sales manager learned that one of their top accounts was part of an HVAC buying group in the New York metro area. Would they be willing to introduce Brookaire to other members of the buying group?

"Of course," said the client. "We love your products. We love your service. We'll make some calls."

The buying group included some of the largest companies in the HVAC industry. All of them had a great deal in common with the original client: They were forward thinking, focused on hiring and retaining a high-caliber technical workforce with training, and offered above-average wages and great benefits. They were not only passionate about their workers, but also their customers, their reputation in their markets, the results they delivered. In short, they were exactly the kind of companies that Brookaire wanted to do business with. Before long, they'd set up appointments with five other members of the buying group, contacts they expected would lead to great business for them.

A no-brainer, right?

But ordinary salespeople don't have a referral strategy. They don't look at referrals as a significant revenue opportunity. Oh, they might ask once in a while, when they remember. But after a few halfhearted attempts, most give up.

They give up because they don't get many referrals when they ask, and the few they get often don't pan out. Plus, salespeople worry that, by asking, they'll put their sales relationship at risk.

It's true that many referrals you talk to aren't actively buying (though sometimes you do get lucky). But that's not the primary goal. Even when they're not in buying mode, referrals offer tremendous value by expanding your network. The person you're referred to may end up referring you to someone else. He or she may open a door for you in the organization. And when a need arises, that person will probably give you a call.

And, yes, it's true that the volume of referrals is low. But what's often overlooked is that the value is extraordinarily high. How many prospects do you have to call to get someone who's willing to have even just a conversation with you? One referral can be worth dozens or even hundreds of ordinary leads.

And most important of all, you've already overcome the greatest barrier in prospecting: lack of trust. When you're cold calling or following up on a marketing lead, the typical response is, "Who are you? Why should I listen to you? Who says so besides you? What can you do for me?"

If referrals aren't worth the trouble, why is it that some of the most successful salespeople have a referral-only business? It's because they're at a point where they don't want or need to chase every lukewarm lead that comes their way. Their time has become so valuable that they can only afford to spend it with high-probability prospects. And referrals are the highest probability prospects you'll ever find.

Successful salespeople also understand that referrals enhance their credibility and perceived value with existing customers. It turns them into a scarce resource. Customers feel like they're part of an exclusive club, and they're doing their friends a favor by inviting them to the club. If you offer extraordinary value to your customers, they can't wait to spread the news.

Your career may not have reached that point yet. But that doesn't diminish the power of referrals, or the value of a *strategy*—a plan to pursue referrals consistently and make them a significant part of your prospecting plan.

DO YOU BELIEVE?

•

When salespeople hesitate to ask for referrals, it tells me that they're not 100 percent convinced that they add value to their customers.

Ultimate Sales Professionals ask for referrals because they believe in what they're selling. They don't think of a referral as a favor bestowed on them by a buyer. It's a win-win for both. Think of when you've had an opportunity to recommend a valued provider—a doctor, a remodeler, a mechanic. You're adding value with a good recommendation.

Here's how USPs get referrals: They ask for them!

They assume and expect they will get referrals. They will ask anyone who could potentially point them to business. They will ask folks who are not in a position to buy or are not interested in buying from them and prospects who don't fit the profile.

I spoke in Chapter Six about Arrowquip, the manufacturer of cattle chutes. It targeted only certain types of equipment dealers—those who were willing and able to sell high-cost, high-value solutions.

Of course, you can't always tell in advance whether a dealer will fit the profile. But if Arrowquip determined that a particular dealer wasn't a good prospect, it didn't let the contact go to waste. They immediately asked for referrals: "Based on what you're telling me, I understand that we're probably not a good fit for you. But perhaps you can point me in the right direction. Which dealers in your area are focused on the premium end of the market?" They were actually asking dealers to refer their competitors! And guess what? Most of the time, they got a name.

It's easy to ask for referrals when you appeal to someone's knowledge, strengths, or qualities. For example: "Alex, you've been in business for more than twenty-five years and have built up quite a reputation with your customers and in the industry. Tell me, who are two or three individuals that you admire and respect, who might be receptive to some ideas on how they can improve/fix/enhance/achieve/eliminate?"

QUALITY ATTRACTS QUALITY

•

The best-of-the-best referrals always come from your best customers—the ones who share your values and beliefs. Quality
attracts quality, and chances are they will be happy to introduce
you to colleagues who are on the same wavelength.

A company that manufactures plastic tanks for specialty
chemicals found me on the internet. It would be hard to
imagine a more unlikely fit. I live in Delaware. They're based in
Neche, North Dakota, population 100. They invited me out to
their facility and, despite our different backgrounds, we hit it off
immediately. I respected their work ethic, their integrity, their
passion for what they did.

When we broke for lunch, the owner pulled me aside. "Just
a heads-up," he warned. "Our community doesn't allow us to
break bread with nonmembers. So I'll set up a separate table
for you to sit by yourself. I hope you're not offended." I wasn't.
When I'm a guest, I respect my host's cultural values and beliefs.

I learned that their religion places a high emphasis on ethical behavior. The bottom line is that I really respected their
beliefs, especially when it came to business. These were the kind
of people I wanted to work with. Evidently they felt the same
way, because even though I wasn't "one of them," we did a lot
of business together. It was unspoken that our beliefs and values
were quite similar. I still can't break bread with them, but we're
family.

As a result, they've opened many doors for me. They felt
comfortable recommending me to their customers and to other
companies they worked with. And it was all based on me being

persistent and asking, "Who do you admire and respect that would be interested in generating more sales and keeping their sales team motivated and focused?" I've asked variations of that question many times over the course of our relationship. I usually get two or three names every time. I've gotten more than twenty major clients through this process, resulting in more than $1 million in fees.

REFERRALS ARE PREQUALIFIED

In Chapter Six, I wrote about profiling. When you're prospecting, it's important to focus on the types of customers who are most likely to buy. Generally, for example, I look for potential clients who meet a certain revenue threshold, who work in certain industries, and who are in certain parts of the country.

But when I get a good referral, these criteria take a back seat. The reason is simple. In general, prospecting is a low-yield activity. The reason you profile is to keep low-potential prospects out of your pipeline. Referral business, by contrast, is highly efficient. When someone makes an introduction, you can bypass all that pick-and-shovel prospecting work. In a sense, you're working with a lead that's been prequalified by the person who gave you the referral.

The clients I've won from my friends in North Dakota prove the point. None of them fit my prospecting profile. None had more than ten salespeople; most only had two or three. Many of the referrals were in industries I didn't have much experience with. Most were geographically undesirable—I had to get on a plane and spend a day or sometimes two to meet with them. That violates all my rules for prospecting.

Why do it? Because these leads are extraordinarily valuable. Even though they're small companies, they spend on average eight times the amount of my "ideal" profile clients. Because they trust me, and because we share values, they tend to engage me for long-term assignments. That's more profitable for me and, more important, allows me to be much more effective for them. There are many more things I can do over a six-month to one-year engagement versus a quick-fix engagement. Consequently, the clients get better results. And when that happens, they bring you back to do more work. And—I'm closing the circle on referrals here—they introduce you to their contacts who want what they're getting.

That's how a referral business works.

21

BE PARANOID

In personal relationships, jealousy is an ugly thing. You don't want to be the suspicious spouse or boyfriend/girlfriend who's always wondering whether your significant other is stepping out on you.

In commercial relationships, like the ones you have with your customers, you *should* be suspicious. Because, let's face it: In business, the rules are different. Buyers may tell you they love you. They might even mean it. But that doesn't mean they won't cheat on you.

And if they do, they probably won't even feel bad about it. After all, it's not like they're *sleeping* around. They're just *shopping* around.

That's why Ultimate Sales Professionals are professionally paranoid. They don't take customers' love for granted. When buyers tell them, "You guys are the best," they take it with a grain of salt. They've seen too many "best" relationships go down the drain in an instant, with no warning. They know that customers will continue to profess their love even while they're negotiating with your competitor, because they don't want you to leave them in a lurch before the new deal is in place. They *assume* that customers are always considering other options. And their radar is constantly searching for the slightest sign of trouble.

Consider my clients Reg and David. They manage a company that manufactures and sells air filters and belts to the HVAC industry. They take a personal approach to their business and their customers. They make a pilgrimage every year right after Thanksgiving, personally delivering gift baskets to top clients. They tell me the baskets work like a charm. Clients get goodies to share with their team. And they're always willing to spend a little quality time with Reg and David, talking about the past year's business and working together in the coming year.

As they were telling me how useful this strategy has been for them, Reg and David pointed out one success in particular: In one of these visits, they learned that one of their best clients was in the process of price shopping, so they were able to deal with the situation.

Alarm bells were going off in my mind. "With all due respect," I said, "why would you consider them a good client if they're shopping around?"

Reg and David looked at each other. "Well, they do a lot of business with us," Reg began.

"That makes them a big customer, not necessarily a good customer," I answered. "In fact, they could end up being a nightmare *because* they do a lot of business with you. You're counting on that business, and if they take it elsewhere you're going to be in deep trouble, right?"

"But they always tell us how much they like working with us," David objected.

"Look at what they do, not what they say," I said. "They say they love you, but they're acting to commoditize you. The fact that they're shopping around means they've already decided they can live without you."

Reg and David had made a classic sales mistake. They'd been lulled into a false sense of security by all the wonderful things their customer was telling them.

As they say, the spouse is always the last one to know.

HOW DO THEY LOVE YOU?
MAKE THEM COUNT THE WAYS

•

Here's what I suggested to Reg and David about engaging their top clients:

During your visits, ask them to reflect on how your company has been delivering value to them. It's a natural and legitimate question. After all, you need to understand how your customers define value.

But the conversation has another purpose as well. There's a well-known principle in psychology known as "cognitive dissonance." People have an intrinsic need to align what they say with what they do, and vice versa. So when you get your clients to articulate your value—to actually say it out loud—their subsequent actions are more likely to align with what they told you. In other words, if you make them *tell* you why they love you, they're more likely to *act* like they love you. They're less likely to shop around, because they're thinking about value, not price. When they've told you about all the ways you're helping them achieve their goals, they're more likely to treat you like the valued partner that you are. They're less likely to commoditize you.

Even better: Ask them to quantify that value. Have they seen an increase in productivity, revenue, reduced expenses, reduced time on the job, better turnaround, quality, or whatever metrics apply to your value proposition?

In short, when customers say nice things about you, ask them to prove it. You might say something like this: "I really appreciate your kind words and how happy you are. Tell me why you say that." Or, "Can you think of a recent example that comes to mind as you reflect on our business over the past year?" You may know the answer already, but when a customer brings the story back to life, they get emotionally attached to it.

It's easy for salespeople to take things for granted, especially when things are going well with a customer. They assume the customer understands the value they're getting or is too sophisticated to get seduced by a low price. Me, I'm jealous. I always assume others are out there looking for a way to steal my customer or their budget. What I do with this info is put it in my pocket. Then, sometime in the future, if and when they push back a little and say "we need to shop around, save some money," I have some reliable, quantifiable information they gave me that I can push back on without getting confrontational. I have to remind them, resell, justify what they justified to me. After all, since that important information came from them, they believe it, and won't refute it.

Of course, this strategy doesn't completely inoculate you from price issues. But if your buyer is feeling some pressure to get lower prices—perhaps at the urging of senior management or because costs are going up elsewhere in the business—he or she is more likely to weigh that against your value, the value your buyer articulated. So, when you get some version of the "we love you, but your price is high" speech, don't get defensive. Simply repeat back to your buyer what he or she told you.

Is this approach manipulative? Are you trying to exploit your buyer by putting them in an uncomfortable psychological position? I don't think so. If you aren't delivering value, this strategy won't work—in fact, it will backfire. But if you *are* doing a good job for them, there's nothing underhanded about taking credit for it. You would do your buyer a disservice to let price be a distraction when what they really want is value.

GET A LITTLE MORE LOVE

●

This tell-me-why-you-love-me discussion also opens up opportunities to do more business with a customer. There's usually some way you can add even more value through an upsell or cross-sell, which benefits both you and the customer. So if a customer loves you, get him to love you even more.

While you're at it, ask if the customer would be willing to serve as a reference or provide you with a testimonial that you can leverage on other sales calls. Stories are powerful, moving, and engaging. Other prospects and customers will hear them and think, "Hey, I want that kind of experience/opportunity, too. How can I get that?"

And one last thing: When customers say they love you—and have just told you all the reasons why—ask for a referral. Why wouldn't they want other people to get the same experience?

22

HIRE A COACH

Since I travel a lot, I need a fitness regimen that can travel with me. I've found that jump-rope is the perfect exercise. No bulky equipment. You can do it anywhere. If the hotel doesn't have a gym, I can do it in the parking lot.

The only problem with jump-rope, as with most forms of exercise, is that the better you get at it the less effective it becomes. You get more efficient, which means you're using less energy. So it's that much harder to get your heart rate up. After a while, you hit a plateau.

That happened to me. So I started looking for some different jump-rope techniques. One, which is popular at cross-fit gyms, is the double-under. You have to speed up the rope so that it passes under your feet *twice* on each jump. It's an intense workout.

After watching a lot of online videos, I gave it a try but couldn't get the rhythm down. After one or two attempts, I was gasping for breath.

"Oh well," I told myself. "This is not for me." I went back to my old routine.

As luck would have it, I came across a jump-rope instructor online, who happened to be hosting a class near me. He demonstrated the technique, had me try it, recorded it, showed me what I did right and what I did wrong. Then we went through it again. By the end of the session, I was managing to get one double-under for every ten attempts or so.

I went back for more sessions. After a month, I could get in a double-under on every fourth or fifth swing of the rope. I kept at it, kept getting feedback and encouragement from my coach, and finally something clicked. After three months, I could do eighty continuous double-unders in a row.

So it turns out you *can* teach an old dog new tricks.

My point, though, is that it's nearly impossible to teach *yourself* new tricks. In sales as in athletics, you reach a plateau. And you need someone who can get you to the next level. Someone who can tell you what you're doing right and what you're doing wrong. Someone you can trust to map out a path to improvement and encourage you to follow it when you're ready to throw in the towel.

LEARNING AND GROWING

•

When I first started out in sales, I was lucky. This was back in prehistoric days. I was just out of college and selling directory advertising for Bell Telephone. They called it "Ma Bell" for a reason. Ma could afford to take care of her children, because they weren't going to leave her. She was the only game in town.

We got four weeks of intensive classroom training before we ever talked to a buyer. Then we got paired up with a sales coach to make calls out in the field. The first two days, the coach took the lead while we watched. It was a good thing; I was so nervous and tongue tied, I couldn't open my mouth. By the third day, I could eke out a few words. Gradually things started clicking.

That level of training eventually went by the wayside. Instead of paying for a dedicated staff of sales coaches, some companies adopted a "mentoring" strategy, which meant the coaching function got offloaded to salespeople. A newbie would be paired up with a seasoned pro who would serve as the mentor. The new hire would shadow the experienced salesperson to learn the ins and outs. They'd meet on a regular basis to brainstorm and review progress.

Some old pros embraced the opportunity to pass on what they'd learned, but let's be real. We're talking about salespeople here. Any time spent mentoring means less time pursuing your own sales. And at the same time that they were being asked to mentor, salespeople were usually being asked to do more with less in other areas. Answer your own phone. Make your own appointments. Fill out your own expense reports. Keep the CRM up to date. Respond to all those emails. Update your projections. Anybody who was asked to be a coach had to think: "It's hard enough trying to do my job and cover my own backside. You think I have time to look out for you? Sorry, pal. You're on your own!"

These days, coaching responsibilities mostly fall on the shoulders of sales managers. Most, I've found, are not good coaches. They're not trained to do it. Too often, they resort to talking or lecturing or pontificating, or relating stories of how they used to do it back in the day. These are easy outs, but you can't entirely blame the manager. They're busy, and effective coaching takes time.

Plus, there's an inherent conflict between the sales manager's main job—hitting the numbers—and the coaching role. In many cases, "coaching" becomes some variation of "Are you hitting your numbers? If not, why not? You need to work harder, make more calls, close more deals. I know you can do it!" Or they coach on what's important to them versus what's relevant to you. If they're getting heat from above because close rates are too low, you're probably going to get coached on closing, even if you know what you really need to work on are relationship-building skills.

The bottom line is you can't rely on your organization to coach or mentor you. Companies are reluctant to invest in training, because who knows how long a salesperson is going to stick around? They might offer some training for new reps to get them up to speed (though it's usually heavy on product training and light on skills). Every now and then they might try to spice things up with a quick dose of canned training. But let's face it—companies are focused on what *they* need. Who's looking out for what *you* need?

When you hire a coach, the coach is working for *you*. Not the company. Not your boss. You can be completely frank with your coach. He or she is not thinking about the company's sales strategy or whether you're making your quota. If there's ever a conflict between what's best for you and what's best for the company, there's no question where your coach's loyalty lies. And if you feel your coach isn't helping you improve your game, you can find a different one.

FINDING A COACH

It's not easy to find a good coach. There aren't many around because there aren't many salespeople hiring them.

It's mind-boggling, really. We hire professionals to help us manage our money, but not to help us make our money. We gladly pay for all kinds of services: people to tailor our clothes, fix our cars, remodel our kitchens, cook and serve our meals. We'll pay for a personal trainer to keep us fit. We'll pay for a therapist to keep us sane. Yet very few people are willing to make a similar investment in their careers.

The reason, I believe, is that so many of us are still stuck in the old employer-employee mind-set. Job training? That's something my employer should offer, not something I should pay for. You might as well ask me to pay for my desk and chair.

That mind-set can be very costly in the long run.

And that's where you, as an Ultimate Sales Professional, have an edge. If you're managing your career while others are just working for a living, who's going to succeed in the end?

Even though I've been conducting sales training and consulting for the past twenty-five years, I hire coaches to critique me, challenge me, and help me grow. I surround myself with people who I believe are more gifted than I am in these areas and who are willing to help me grow and adapt to change.

I pay them enough to make the relationship worth their while. It's not an insignificant sum, but it's in line with what I pay for other professional services. What I get in return is someone whose judgment I trust; someone I can reach out to whenever I need a fresh set of eyes on a problem I'm facing; someone who won't be afraid to tell me when I'm about to make a mistake; someone who can get me unstuck when I'm stuck and take me from where I am to where I want to be.

WHAT TO LOOK FOR IN A COACH

•

Where do you find such a person? The best way, I've found, is through word of mouth and old-fashioned networking. It's similar to finding an accountant, real estate agent, physician, or other professional. You start by asking around. Or doing a Google search. Of course you'll ask about experience, track record, and references. Ask for examples of how they helped their clients with similar challenges and the results they achieved. Ask about their own sales experience and accomplishments.

Here are some questions you can ask:

- What is your philosophy on selling, especially as it relates to what I sell?

- What are some past success stories you've had with other clients, especially ones that are similar to the industry I sell?
- What is your past background in selling? Your credentials, certifications with coaching?
- How do you typically work with clients when it comes to coaching, motivating, supporting, and keeping the client accountable toward his or her goals?
- How long is the coaching commitment?
- If I am not satisfied with the coaching after __ weeks, can I cancel?
- Do you do in-person coaching or in-the-field joint sales calls on some of my accounts?
- What support material, resources, and tools will you provide beyond our coaching sessions that I can access to ensure my success?
- To what extent will you role-play with me to get me comfortable in the skill set?
- How accessible are you, especially if I need a fast answer or I'm facing a problem between our coaching sessions?

Remember that a coach is not a guru. Great coaches don't have all the answers. What they're really good at is asking questions—questions that help *you* find the answers that work for you. Their real value is to offer an outside perspective, especially in situations where you're too close to the problem. What you want is someone who can listen, brainstorm, get you to think, help you make a plan and hold you accountable to a plan.

It's best to speak with several candidates to get a sense of their approach and how you might work together. Most sales coaches will offer a complimentary session so you can try them out. After you've chosen a coach, remember that you're not locked in. Establish a trial period to see if the relationship works. If you're not feeling it, end the relationship gracefully and keep looking.

The most important thing is to set clear goals and expectations up front. Do you want feedback on your selling skills? Do you want someone who can help you start pursuing bigger opportunities? Do you need someone to hold you accountable for prospecting? Or do you need someone to help you navigate specific sales situations as they arise? Be sure you and your coach both understand the rules of engagement and what you want to accomplish. Write down the goals and, if you can, create metrics and a timetable. Coaching works best when the goals are clear. Remember my jump-rope coach? We were perfectly in sync about what I wanted.

WHAT TO WORK ON WITH YOUR COACH

•

You've no doubt learned the basics of selling by now (though it's amazing what we forget over time). For experienced pros, the challenges are different from reps just starting out: They have so much knowledge and experience that it can get in the way. They can end up talking too much, talking down to buyers, getting impatient, or jumping to conclusions. Or they lose focus and discipline.

When you're just starting out in sales, it can be terrifying. So you overprepare. You rehearse your sales presentation repeatedly. You write out every question you think a buyer might ask, as well as your responses. You ask buyers lots and lots of questions, because you don't know anything. You're constantly trying different sales techniques and ideas, because you don't know what works.

But as you get better at your job, what happens? You don't need to rehearse your presentation; you've given it dozens of times. You don't ask the buyer as many questions; you know that most of your prospects face the same kinds of business challenges. You don't look for new sales techniques, because you've found ones that work.

You get sloppy. You start cutting corners. Even though you know better, you allow unqualified buyers into your pipeline. You skimp on sales discovery. You talk too much and listen too little. You try to close before you've established value.

It's so hard to see these behaviors from the inside out. It's like when I was trying to learn how to double-under on my own. I was so busy trying to do it that I couldn't see what I was doing wrong.

PEER COACHING

If you're not ready to hire a personal coach, or you're having trouble finding one, an alternative to consider is a peer coach. Find another salesperson whose skills and judgment you trust—or a small group—and coach one another. Peer feedback can be as effective as a professional coach, perhaps more so, because they're facing the same issues as you. A peer coach might be a current or former colleague. In some organizations, salespeople meet with one another—without the boss present—to share ideas and problem-solve. It might be a person or group of like-minded people that you connect with through a trade organization or a networking event. A lot of people find good groups on LinkedIn and Facebook.

Or it might be someone who sells a similar, but noncompetitive, product or service to similar types of buyers. For example, if you're primarily selling services to Fortune 500 companies, connect with others who sell other kinds of services to the Fortune 500 companies. Perhaps you sell benefits consulting and your counterpart sells IT support services. You sell different things and target different buyers. But you still face similar challenges, navigating the ins and outs of a large organization, dealing with purchasing departments, identifying decision makers, and so on. So you understand each other's worlds.

Whether you hire a personal coach or engage in more informal peer coaching, it's not really about finding someone who can teach you things you don't know. The real value of a coach is to supply that outside perspective—to ask good questions, to get you to do the things you know you should be doing but aren't. A coach keeps you honest with yourself, helps you see where you might be cutting corners in your sales process, for example, or points out blind spots that might be holding you back. A good coach helps you think.

23

DO THE THING YOU DON'T
WANT TO DO

When I was with Dale Carnegie training, we got a call one day
from a senior executive at a well-known financial institution in
greater Philadelphia. She said she wanted to take the class. We
scheduled a meeting so I could learn more about what she was
looking to get out of the course.

When we met, I was immediately impressed. Often people
came to us because they're rough around the edges: a plant manager who inadvertently makes the rank and file workers angry,
or the owner of a family business who's rude and insulting to
the staff. This executive was different. She was polished, fluent,
gracious, empathetic. It seemed clear to me that she already had
outstanding leadership skills. So, I asked: "Why are you coming
to us? Why do you want to go through this program?"

She said: "Well, a year ago, the president of the bank decided to retire. I was offered the position. But I turned it down."

"Wait a minute," I said. "Why would you turn down an opportunity like that? Especially if they came to you?"

"Here's the thing," she said. "I'm very comfortable working with people one-on-one and in small groups. But I absolutely hate speaking in large groups and public venues. And I'm bad at it. If I were president of the bank, I'd be speaking to boards, the community, and on TV and radio. I just don't have the confidence to speak in public."

Wow. My respect for her grew even more.

She continued: "It's a problem I've been avoiding for a long time. I've managed to work around it by taking jobs where I'm working behind the scenes with my team. But I can't hide from it anymore. In all other respects, I know I could run a bank. But if I can't learn to be more comfortable presenting on my feet, I've gone as far as I can go."

She signed up for a twelve-week public speaking program and did extraordinarily well, as I knew she would.

We kept in touch. Nine months later, she called me with some exciting news.

"Remember when I told you I'd turned down the president's job?" she said. "Well, the person they hired for the job isn't working out. The board approached me again to see if I'd be interested. And guess what? I said yes!"

Here was an individual who had already achieved great success in her career. She was making lots of money, doing a job she loved, and had earned the respect of her people. Life was good. Most people in her position would have been happy to stay in their comfort zone. She really didn't need to force herself to do something that she hated to do. She didn't need to take on something new and risk failing at it. Yet she did.

It wasn't just to get the president's job—remember, when she came to us she'd already turned it down and had no expectation that it would be offered again. It's just who she was. She wanted to push herself to be the best she could be.

LIVING IN THE COMFORT ZONE

•

Most of the people I've worked with, I'm sad to say, don't have that drive. They want to live in their comfort zone. If they achieve some success, they use it to get even deeper into their comfort zone. "I always hated cold calling/coaching/missionary sales/etc.," they say. "I was lousy at it. So now that I've got steady accounts/a promotion/seniority/etc., I don't have to do it anymore. Someone else can do the grunt work. I'll focus on what I'm good at."

I've seen it over and over. Working outside the comfort zone is considered "paying your dues." Let the new person do it; I don't have to anymore.

Ultimate Sales Professionals take a different view. They understand that *their best opportunities lie outside their comfort zone.* They're uncomfortable with being comfortable, because it means they're stagnating. They're drawn to learn how to do the things they're not good at, because that's how they grow. Instead of using success to buy more comfort, they use it to buy more challenges. Because of their success, they can afford to take a chance on something new. If they fail, they can always go back to what they know.

Every time you move out of your comfort zone and succeed, you feel invincible. Every time you do something you didn't think you could do, you can't wait to tackle the next thing. It's building confidence to take on new challenges and resilience to persist despite those challenges.

That's what keeps USPs energized and moving forward long after others have found a safe place to wait out what's left of their careers. I've seen USPs in their fifties and sixties taking on new challenges. They become masters of social media. When their comfortable world gets disrupted by new technology or new business models, they don't try to ride it out to the end; they change what they sell or how they sell.

FACING YOUR FEARS

•

Conventional wisdom can reinforce the desire to stay in your comfort zone. For example, legendary sales trainer Brian Tracy, author of more than thirty business books, says you should focus on your strengths, not your weaknesses.

I take his point, but only to a point.

Yes, you should absolutely focus on your strengths. If you're good at one thing, it makes no sense to abandon it for something else. Your strengths are money in the bank. It's where you get the best return on your effort.

But you shouldn't focus *only* on your strengths. Going outside your comfort zone means *building* on your strengths. Redeploying them in new ways. Identifying the impediments that are keeping you from using them to their greatest effect. My client wasn't abandoning her banking career to become a motivational speaker. She was filling a gap.

The thing that keeps people in their comfort zone is fear. Faced with the unfamiliar, people tend to overestimate the risks and underestimate the rewards. They stick with what they know, or what they think is safe.

It can be incredibly liberating to face your fears. Once you acknowledge them and drag them out into the clear light of day, they're usually more manageable than you thought. It took real guts for my client to admit that she was afraid of public speaking. Over the years, she'd expended a lot of energy *not* confronting those fears, by navigating her career away from situations where she'd be forced to speak in public. But once she faced up to her fear, what happened? She cut it down to size. Instead of something to run away from, it simply became a problem to solve.

What fears are holding you back? What's the thing you know you need to do, but don't want to do? For some, it's prospecting for new business. For others, it's calling on high-level executives, or asking for the sale. Some are afraid of conflict, so they won't demand what they deserve from their boss or company. Or they're afraid of losing an account, so they can't say no when a buyer demands outrageous concessions.

Of the 200,000 professionals I've worked with to date, just about everyone has a skill or aptitude deficit. Call it a weakness,

THE ULTIMATE SALES PRO

a phobia, an inferiority complex when it comes to that one function. You don't have to fix every deficit; most of us find ways to
work around our gaps. But when the deficits are in areas that
are central to our profession, the costs of these workarounds can
be dreadful. When we find the courage to admit our deficits, or
when circumstances finally force us to do so, many of us feel a
burden being lifted.

When you feel that gnawing in the pit of your stomach
because you're doing the thing you don't want to do, celebrate
the feeling. It means you're breaking new ground.

And if you fail, so what? In business, failure comes with the
territory. I'm not talking about betting the farm. But if you're
pushing yourself outside your comfort zone, it's seldom an
all-or-none proposition. Even if you fail, you still have your core
strengths to rely on.

Imagine the worst thing that could happen to you if you make
that cold call and get rejected. Or get a meeting with a CEO and
end up tongue tied. Life goes on. I have a friend who launched
his own business when he was thirty-two. Unfortunately, the
economy tanked right after he and his partner hung out their
shingle. Business they'd counted on never materialized. And
even when they started making money, he couldn't deal with the
uneven cash flow. He had a young family to support, and he was
the only breadwinner.

His wasn't a success story. Eventually he shut down the business and went back to the corporate world. Had he failed?
Maybe. But in my view, experience is never wasted. He was better
at his job because he'd acquired a deep-down understanding of
how business worked and the challenges that his clients were
facing. And he was inoculated by the failure. The worst had

happened, and he'd survived. Today, many years later, he has a healthy respect for failure. But he doesn't fear it. He's willing to take a risk when the circumstances call for it.

USPs have to be proactive, recognize what skill they need to grow, embrace the deficit, address it, work it, stretch it, and finally master it so it becomes an asset instead of a liability.

24

STEPPING OFF THE EDGE

I've had my own business for nearly twenty years.

I wish I could tell you that I had such confidence in my dreams and goals that I just closed my eyes, quit my day job, and sailed off into the wild blue yonder.

The truth is, I got pushed.

Several years before I launched my business, I'd been recruited to start a sales training division for a major publishing firm. It was a pretty scary proposition. The company had never done anything like it before. On the other hand, they had a huge subscriber base and marketing department that could supply virtually endless leads. And the starting salary wasn't bad either.

It was a lot of fun building a business from the ground up, and we made good progress at first. After several years, however, growth started to slow down. The company's customer base was primarily individual salespeople and small companies, while we needed to reach larger companies with significant training budgets. And the marketing department was designed around quick, transactional sales, not the consultative selling approach needed for selling training programs. I couldn't convince the CEO to try a different strategy. Everything I proposed, he shot down. He was focused on the core publishing business, which at the time was highly profitable.

I felt I'd learned enough at this point to start my own business, but with my wife home as a full-time mom to our two-year-old and four-year-old, I needed to be cautious. While I was considering my options and trying to lay the groundwork, the decision was made for me.

One day I arrived at work, got pulled into the office of the human resources director, and was told, "Today's your last day."

Even when you should see it coming, it's still a shock. I figured I'd have enough time and advance notice to engineer a smooth transition, and possibly negotiate to take some accounts with me. Nope. A severance package to tide me over? Nope. What about my wife and children? Sorry.

I was home by lunchtime. That afternoon, I was making phone calls.

It turned out that my security blanket—my former company's name and resources, and that steady paycheck—had been a straitjacket. With nobody but myself to answer to, I was free to sell the way I wanted, to the people I wanted. Twelve months later, I'd doubled my business.

My only regret was that my boss didn't give me the boot sooner. A swift kick in the ass kept me focused on my dreams.

WHAT'S YOUR DREAM?

•

That was my dream—to run my own sales training business. I was lucky enough to be successful at it.

Of course, I'm not suggesting that self-employment is the path for everyone. It's not even for most people. But whatever your ultimate dream is, you're going to have to take some risks to get there. Maybe it's a job with a different company. Maybe it's a move into a management role. Maybe it's winning accounts that now seem out of reach. Or doubling your income. Whatever your dream is, you can't get there by doing the same old same old. To achieve something you've never achieved before, you need to do something you've never done before. There are no guarantees that you'll be successful. But you'll never know whether you can fly unless you step off the edge.

Describe your dream as vividly as you can. What is your role? What are you selling? Who are your customers? How much money are you making? What kind of impact are you having on your customers? What do customers say about you? How does your competition react when they hear your name? How would you like to be remembered as a sales professional?

Next, describe in detail the action steps you need to get there. For example, if your dream is to be the go-to expert in your field, what steps do you need to take to acquire that expertise? And what steps will you take to demonstrate that knowledge to customers and prospects?

START PREPARING NOW

•

Was I prepared to start my own business? It sure didn't feel like it. But when push came to shove, so to speak, it turned out I had what I needed to get started.

That said, the transition could have been easier if I'd done more to get ready. Whatever your dream is, there are plenty of things you can start doing now to get yourself in the best possible position to succeed. If you want to be an industry guru, you don't have to quit your job to start learning what you need to know. If you want to enhance your personal brand, you can start writing articles and speaking at conferences right now.

These steps do require time and effort. Your current employer may not support them. You may have to do them on your own time and spend your own money. But the good news is that they will pay dividends even before you make the leap. They'll make you better at the job you have.

Be careful, however, that preparation doesn't become an excuse for inaction. I had a million reasons to put off launching my own business: I should get more money in the bank. Wait until the kids were older, or my wife went back to work. Wait until the economy improved, or my business cards were printed, or my business plan was written. The truth is, I was scared. Lucky for me, I couldn't wait any longer.

SUGGESTIONS FOR SOLO PRACTITIONERS

•

If working for yourself is part of your dream, here are some suggestions I can offer (with the benefit of hindsight):

You need something to sell. Are you selling your own expertise as a consultant? Are you selling someone else's services? Selling products as an independent rep? Whatever it is, personal selling works best with higher-value products. As a solo practitioner, it's hard to make a living grinding out lots of little sales.

You need money to buy time. Most new businesses are under-capitalized, because it takes time to build a pipeline. For example, if your typical sales cycle is six months, that's how long it will be before you can expect to see your first check, and even longer until you see a regular cash flow. The biggest risk is that if you're desperate for cash in the early days, you can end up making bad deals and decisions that will haunt you later. So make sure you can afford to wait. That doesn't necessarily mean that you need enough money to maintain your current lifestyle during the dry period (though that would be ideal). Know where you can cut your current expenses quickly if necessary. For example, could you sell your car and lease to free up cash flow? If you've been living on two incomes, can you live on one for a while?

You still need a tribe. In other chapters (see Chapter Three), we've talked about the importance of belonging to the right tribe. If you're going out on your own, that's truer than ever. You'll be losing your employer's tribe, so other connections are that much more important. Before you make the leap, network like never before. Not just potential prospects. Connect with people who can refer business to you, speak up for you, help you solve problems, be a resource when you need one.

Focus on the essentials. These days, you really don't need much infrastructure to run your business. You don't need an answering service; you have a cell phone. You probably don't need an office, just a laptop. If you need to set up a meeting, consider co-working space. Or meet in a restaurant. Or come to the customer. You don't even need a car—you can use Lyft, rent a car, get a ZipCar. People get caught up in the need to look like a "legitimate" business, but few of your prospects will care. It's a virtual world, and everybody is used to it. In sales, your most valuable asset is between your ears.

Be careful about partnering. It's lonely out there, and it may feel safer to partner up with someone else. That's often a big mistake, especially if you're partnering with someone whose skill set duplicates yours. Feeding two mouths is a lot harder than feeding one, especially if you both do the same kinds of things.

Build a business model. Act like a real company where it counts: Have a business plan. Set revenue goals and projections. Breakeven points. Go/no go decision points. Lots of people stick with something too long because they're afraid to define what will constitute success and failure. You need to know if you're failing—not so you can throw in the towel, but so you can make adjustments. For example, if your model is based on generating $100K gross revenue per quarter, and after six months you're averaging $75K, you know what your gap is. You may just need a few tweaks to close that gap. But if you're only doing $25K, you'll need to take a hard look at your assumptions and change your strategy.

Have a prospecting/marketing plan. Once you've worked through your personal contacts, how are you going to attract new customers? It's easy to fall into the trap of acquiring a few clients and then spending all your time servicing them. That usually ends badly. You need to have a plan to keep filling the bucket.

Be ethical. Don't steal customer lists from your former employer or violate your noncompete agreement. Don't solicit business for yourself on your employer's time. Don't tell prospects you have ten employees when you don't. Unethical behavior gets very expensive very quickly. When you're launching a business, you need to focus all of your time and resources on it. You can't afford lawsuits from former employers or complaints from angry customers who feel you weren't straight with them.

I'm the first to admit that running your own business isn't easy. The upside for me is that I'm responsible for my own success. I get to build the kind of business I want, without asking someone else's permission. I can focus on my clients and provide great service rather than navigate the politics of a large organization. I don't have to worry about my boss getting jealous of my success, cutting my commissions, reassigning my best accounts, or moving me to Duluth.

For me, the rewards are worth the risk. I did need a push. But I only needed one. I've never gone back.

Again, this path isn't for everyone. In a sense, however, this entire book is about working for yourself. Whether you own your own business, or you're one of hundreds of reps in a large company; no matter what it says on your business card, or who issues your paycheck—if you're in sales, you're working for yourself. I know reps who've been out on their own and successful but go back on the inside when the right opportunity comes up.

And in the modern economy, the line between the two is increasingly fuzzy. The good thing about being an Ultimate Sales Professional is you're developing the skills and knowledge that will prepare you to succeed in either situation. To me, that's the most liberating idea of all. It means *you* have the freedom to choose how to reach your goals.

25

STAND BY YOUR VALUES

One of the things that has long bothered me about the state of modern business is a widespread sense of casual expediency when it comes to ethics and values. I'm not suggesting that businesspeople should aspire to sainthood. The marketplace can get rough. There are winners and losers. Businesses fail. People lose their jobs. Accounts go south. Priorities change. Expectations aren't met. All that comes with the territory. Nor am I suggesting that people should put the interests of others ahead of their own. We're all working hard to provide for ourselves and those we love. If you don't look out for Number One, who will? I have no problem with any of that.

What I'm talking about is the willingness of some people to navigate these difficult waters without a set of guiding principles.

Companies and individuals who cut corners for a quick buck. Promises made and later broken. The idea that lies told in business don't count. "Oh, I shipped that order out last week. I'm surprised you didn't get it yet." (*It's sitting on my desk.*) "Oh, I'm so sorry. Your invoice fell between the cracks." (*The CFO is slow-paying all invoices this month.*) "That deal is practically in the bag, Boss. (*I need to call them and see what's up.*) "If you come work for us, you can easily earn six figures in your first year." (*It's never happened yet, but who knows?*)

There are plenty of excuses for such behavior: "All reps inflate their projections; I'm just leveling the playing field." "What the client doesn't know won't hurt him." "When I fudge my expense report, it makes up for all the times I forgot to get a receipt." "I never told the prospect that my competitor is in financial trouble; I simply raised the question." And the most common one of all: "Who cares?"

Who cares? Customers. Colleagues. Employers. They may not call you on it. They may even agree with you that "everyone does it." But they notice. And they remember.

And when they encounter a vendor, coworker, or employee who holds him- or herself to a higher standard of integrity, they notice and remember that, too.

USPs play hard, but they play fair. They understand that, in the end, their trustworthiness is their stock in trade. And they won't sell it out, even if it costs them a sale, a customer, or a job.

TRUTH

•

USPs traffic in truth. They don't tell the customer what he or she wants to hear. They don't say yes to everything. They don't promise the moon. They don't spin. They tell the truth.

Obviously you damage long-term relationships and repeat business when you're less than forthright, or when you over-promise. But average salespeople are sometimes too willing to take that hit in exchange for short-term gain. "First I gotta get the sale," they think. "I'll deal with the rest down the road."

Such sales come at a steep price. You risk more than a customer's dissatisfaction. If they feel betrayed by you, they will make it a priority to punish you. They'll rat you out to anyone who will listen—colleagues in their company, their counterparts in other companies, even their competitors. If your name or your company's name comes up in casual conversation, they'll make a point of telling everyone that you're a snake and not to be trusted.

CRISIS POINTS

•

Sooner or later, every salesperson will face one or more crisis points where the pressure to compromise their ethics and beliefs is almost irresistible. I don't want to minimize the difficulty of such moments. And I'm certainly in no position to judge. None of us is perfect. We've all made choices that we were uncomfortable with and done things even though we knew better. Sometimes we get away with it; sometimes we don't. All I can suggest is that we be honest with ourselves when we don't live up to our principles and ethics, learn from our experiences, and vow to do better in the future.

I will say that one of the best things about the fast pace of business these days is that it's forgiving of mistakes. The world moves on quickly. It's rare indeed that the consequences of doing the difficult-but-right thing are as catastrophic as we fear.

Case in point: I once worked with a talented colleague. I was a newbie; she was experienced and taught me the ropes. She was generous with her time, advice, and encouragement.

After a few months, it became clear that she was getting a raw deal from management because of her gender. I was getting assignments, leads, and even existing accounts that rightfully belonged to her. I was the fair-haired boy. I got spiffs that my colleague wasn't getting. I'd see the boss belittle her for no reason. Her numbers declined because she wasn't getting the same opportunities as I was. It became evident that the boss was hoping that if he made her life miserable enough, she'd quit.

She didn't quit. She sued for discrimination. I decided to come forward and testify on her behalf. I think my employer was surprised. After all, in many ways, I'd been the beneficiary of their unfair treatment of her.

I knew that this would be the end of my career at the company. They couldn't fire either of us in the short run without it looking like retaliation, but I knew they'd be gunning for me soon enough. I'll admit it was difficult to speak up against my boss. Personally, he'd treated me well and we had good rapport. You don't want to feel like you're biting the hand that feeds you. And I did worry whether word would get out to other employers and I'd be tagged as a troublemaker. But I felt good about doing the right thing and resolved to let the chips fall where they would.

I'm glad I did. I found another job. Life went on. And I still had my integrity.

INDEX

confidence, 98
consultations, free, 107–109
consulting business, xii
corporate ladder, xv
cost-cutting pressures, xvii
counterfeit parts, 118
credentials, 4
customer needs, identifying, xxii
customers
    connecting with, 138
    internal, 127–131
    most important, 129
    relationships with, 41–43
    responsiveness to, 60–61
    salesperson as advocate, 49–52
    tactics, 79
customers' organizations,
        relationships, xix

Dale Carnegie, 5–6, 15
dealers, assumptions about,
        37–38
decision maker, selling to, 85–92
Diogenes, 86
directory advertising, xvii, xxi
Donnelly (Yellow Book), xvii
downtime, cost of, 70, 71
dreams, 2, 177
drivers, and success, xvi

efficiency, 30, 32
elevator speeches, 140–141
emotions, xix
ethics, 181, 183–187
executives, sales appointments
        with, 87
expectations, 22
    buyers vs. sellers, 105

failing forward, 7–8
failure, 2, 172
familiarity, vs. competence, 100

fears, facing, 170–173
Federal Aviation Administration,
        118
focus, xiv
    on ideal customer, 39
follow-up
    attempts, and sales success, 31
    schedule for, 56
food store chains, selling to, 89
foundational skills, xx–xxii
Frameco, customer profile,
        34–35
free items, and value, 106–107
freelancers, 66

giving and getting, 100–113
goals, xxiv, 1–8
    for coaching, 164
    questions about, 47
    setting your own, 19–23
growth, 169–170

high-level decision makers, sales
        to, 88–89
honesty, 3, 48, 80

ideas, selling, 3
industry, xix
    move to new, 13–14
information gathering, 96–97
insurance industry, 32–34
internet, xvii
introductions, asking for, 45–46

job skills, xxi
job termination, 176
jump-rope, 157–158

"knowing" skills
    knowing how, xx–xxii
    knowing whom, xviii–xix
    knowing why, xxiii–xxiv, 9–11

ABOUT THE AUTHOR

Paul Cherry is Founder of Performance Based Results (PBResults.com), which specializes in customer engagement strategies to win more sales. He has worked with more than 1,200 organizations in every major industry and has been featured in more than 250 publications, including *Inc.*, *Investor's Business Daily*, *Selling Power*, and *Kiplinger's*. Paul is the author of *Questions That Sell*. He lives near Philadelphia.